IDEA®
Picture
Dictionary

An IDEA® Language Development Resource

BALLARD
&TIGHE
PUBLISHERS

Brea, California

Phonics Consultant

Dr. Norma Inabinette received her doctorate in education and psychology from the University of Buffalo. She is a professor emeritus at California State University, Fullerton. Her 27-year teaching career included a specialization in the diagnosis of reading disabilities and remedial instruction. She also directed the campus reading clinic, providing instruction to community members with reading disabilities. She currently conducts staff development and consults with school districts, publishers, and community agencies throughout Southern California.

Language Development Consultant

Bonnie McKenna received her teaching credential from the University of California, Riverside and her TESL certificate and CLAD credential from the University of California, Irvine. She has been an educator for more than thirty years, working as an elementary-level teacher, a college lecturer, and a teacher of adult ESL. She currently teaches and develops curriculum for the Community Based English Tutoring (CBET) program in the Capistrano Unified School District in California. She was one of the first teachers to pioneer the CBET program in 1999.

Reviewers

The *IDEA Picture Dictionary* greatly benefited from the educators who carefully reviewed the dictionary and provided helpful comments and suggestions.

> Patricia Amaya-Thetford, Alcott Elementary School, Pomona, California
> Gilda Bazan-Lopez, Educational Consultant, Houston, Texas
> Beverly Crowe, Gallup-McKinley County Public Schools, Gallup, New Mexico
> Gretchen Gross, Yuma District #1, Yuma, Arizona
> Dr. Joyce Lancaster, Educational Consultant, Tampa, Florida
> Robyn Ospital, La Habra City School District, La Habra, California
> Dr. Betsy Rymes, University of Georgia, Athens, Georgia
> Dr. Patricia Sanchez-Diaz, Parent Consultant, Menlo Park, California
> Karen Shaw, Educational Consultant, Brea, California
> Caryn Sonberg, Cora Kelly Magnet School, Alexandria, Virginia
> Ann Stekelberg, Majestic Way Elementary School, San Jose, California
> Dr. Connie Williams, Educational Consultant, Menlo Park, California

Translators

Providing the *IDEA Picture Dictionary* words in six different languages would not have been possible without the talents and dedication of the following translators: Bob Batson, David Brisco, David Goetz, George Hsieh, Chue Lao, Leonor Morris, Cathy Sanchez, and Omega Translation Service.

An IDEA® Language Development Resource

Managing Editor: Laurie Regan
Editor: Dr. Roberta Stathis
Editorial Staff: Kristin Belsher, Veronica Jauriqui, and Allison Mangrum
Program Consultants: Virginia Andrade, David Brisco, and Patrice Sonberg Gotsch
Desktop Publishing Coordinator: Kathleen Styffe
Graphic Designers: George Hsieh, Joseph Montoya, and Charles W. Shaffer, III
Printing Coordinator: Cathy Sanchez
Contributing Artists: Gina Capaldi, Sabrina Lammé, and Leilani Trollinger

Printed in the United States of America
ISBN 0-15-338188-4

480 Atlas Street • Brea, CA 92821 • (800) 321-4332 • www.ballard-tighe.com • e-mail: info@ballard-tighe.com

IDEA® Picture Dictionary

Contents

How to use

This shows **how to write** the letter.

These are **guide words**. Guide words tell you the first and last words on the page.

airplane / ant

The words are in **ABC order**.

A
B
C
D
E
F
G
H
I
J
K
L
M
N
O
P
Q
R
S
T
U
V
W
X
Y
Z

airplane (AYR-playn)

Spanish: aeroplano, avión   **Pilipino:** aeroplano

Vietnamese: phi cơ   **Chinese:** 飞机 / 飛機

Hmong: dav hlau   **French:** avion

alligator (AL-uh-gay-tur)

Spanish: cocodrilo   **Pilipino:** buwaya

Vietnamese: cá sấu   **Chinese:** 鳄鱼 / 鱷魚

Hmong: kheb   **French:** alligator

ambulance (AM-byoo-luns)

Spanish: ambulancia   **Pilipino:** ambulansiya

Vietnamese: xe cứu thương   **Chinese:** 救护车 / 救護車

Hmong: tsheb thauj mob   **French:** ambulance

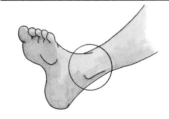

ankle (ANG-kul)

Spanish: tobillo   **Pilipino:** bukung-bukong

Vietnamese: mắt cá   **Chinese:** 脚脖子,踝 / 腳踝

Hmong: pob taws   **French:** cheville

ant (ant)

Spanish: hormiga   **Pilipino:** langgam

Vietnamese: con kiến   **Chinese:** 蚂蚁 / 螞蟻

Hmong: ntsaum   **French:** fourmi

6

4

this dictionary:

This is a **fun activity** for you to try.

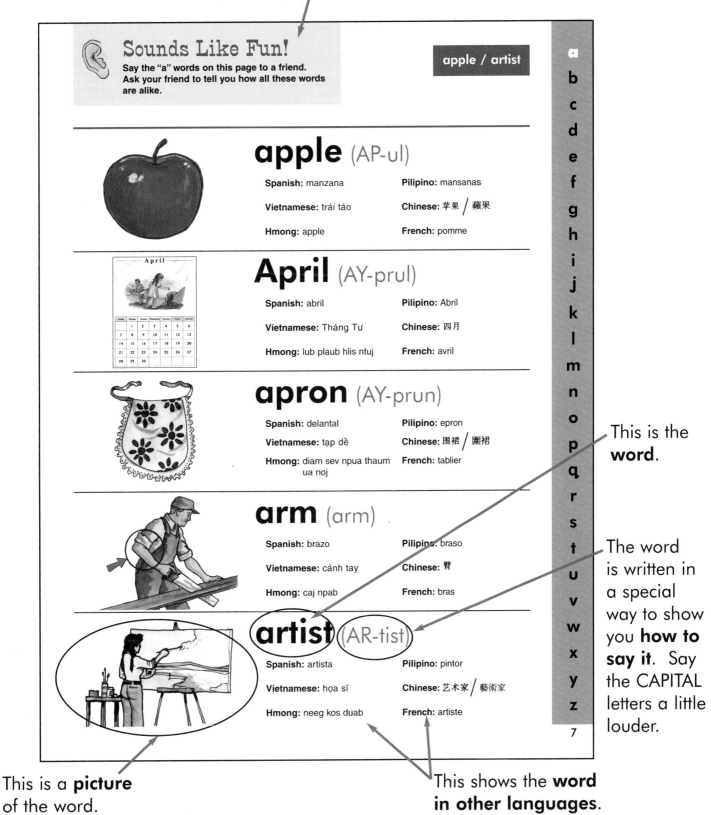

Sounds Like Fun!

Say the "a" words on this page to a friend. Ask your friend to tell you how all these words are alike.

apple (AP-ul)

Spanish: manzana

Pilipino: mansanas

Vietnamese: trái táo

Chinese: 苹果 / 蘋果

Hmong: apple

French: pomme

April (AY-prul)

Spanish: abril

Pilipino: Abril

Vietnamese: Tháng Tư

Chinese: 四月

Hmong: lub plaub hlis ntuj

French: avril

apron (AY-prun)

Spanish: delantal

Pilipino: epron

Vietnamese: tạp dề

Chinese: 围裙 / 圍裙

Hmong: diam sev npua thaum ua noj

French: tablier

arm (arm)

Spanish: brazo

Pilipino: braso

Vietnamese: cánh tay

Chinese: 臂

Hmong: caj npab

French: bras

artist (AR-tist)

Spanish: artista

Pilipino: pintor

Vietnamese: họa sĩ

Chinese: 艺术家 / 藝術家

Hmong: neeg kos duab

French: artiste

This is the **word**.

The word is written in a special way to show you **how to say it**. Say the CAPITAL letters a little louder.

This is a **picture** of the word.

This shows the **word in other languages**.

a b c d e f g h i j k l m n o p q r s t u v w x y z

7

5

AaAa

airplane (AYR-playn)

Spanish: aeroplano, avión

Pilipino: aeroplano

Vietnamese: phi cơ

Chinese: 飞机 / 飛機

Hmong: dav hlau

French: avion

alligator (AL-uh-gay-tur)

Spanish: cocodrilo

Pilipino: buwaya

Vietnamese: cá sấu

Chinese: 鳄鱼 / 鱷魚

Hmong: kheb

French: alligator

ambulance (AM-byoo-luns)

Spanish: ambulancia

Pilipino: ambulansiya

Vietnamese: xe cứu thương

Chinese: 救护车 / 救護車

Hmong: tsheb thauj mob

French: ambulance

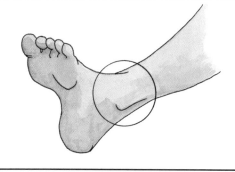

ankle (ANG-kul)

Spanish: tobillo

Pilipino: bukung-bukong

Vietnamese: mắt cá

Chinese: 脚脖子,踝 / 腳踝

Hmong: pob taws

French: cheville

ant (ant)

Spanish: hormiga

Pilipino: langgam

Vietnamese: con kiến

Chinese: 蚂蚁 / 螞蟻

Hmong: ntsaum

French: fourmi

Sounds Like Fun!

Say the "a" words on this page to a friend.
Ask your friend to tell you how all these words
are alike.

apple (AP-ul)

Spanish: manzana

Pilipino: mansanas

Vietnamese: trái táo

Chinese: 苹果 / 蘋果

Hmong: apple

French: pomme

April (AY-prul)

Spanish: abril

Pilipino: Abril

Vietnamese: Tháng Tư

Chinese: 四月

Hmong: lub plaub hlis ntuj

French: avril

apron (AY-prun)

Spanish: delantal

Pilipino: epron

Vietnamese: tạp dề

Chinese: 围裙 / 圍裙

Hmong: diam sev npua thaum ua noj

French: tablier

arm (arm)

Spanish: brazo

Pilipino: braso

Vietnamese: cánh tay

Chinese: 臂

Hmong: caj npab

French: bras

artist (AR-tist)

Spanish: artista

Pilipino: pintor

Vietnamese: họa sĩ

Chinese: 艺术家 / 藝術家

Hmong: neeg kos duab

French: artiste

a
b
c
d
e
f
g
h
i
j
k
l
m
n
o
p
q
r
s
t
u
v
w
x
y
z

astronaut (AS-truh-naht)

Spanish: astronauta

Pilipino: astronaut

Vietnamese: phi hành gia

Chinese: 太空人

Hmong: tus neeg mus saum ntuj

French: astronaute

August (AH-gust)

Spanish: agosto

Pilipino: Agosto

Vietnamese: Tháng Tám

Chinese: 八月

Hmong: yim hli ntuj

French: août

aunt (ant)

Spanish: tía

Pilipino: tiya

Vietnamese: cô, dì

Chinese: 伯母,叔母,姑妈,姨妈／伯母,叔母,姑媽,姨媽

Hmong: phauj, niam tais hlob, niam tais luas, niam dab laug, niam hlob, niam ntxawm

French: tante

axe (aks)

Spanish: hacha

Pilipino: palakol

Vietnamese: cái rìu

Chinese: 斧

Hmong: taus

French: hache

Bb Bb

baby (BAY-bee)

Spanish: bebé   **Pilipino:** sanggol

Vietnamese: em bé   **Chinese:** 婴儿 / 嬰兒

Hmong: me nyuam mos liab   **French:** bébé

back (bak)

Spanish: espalda   **Pilipino:** likod

Vietnamese: cái lưng   **Chinese:** 背

Hmong: nrob qaum   **French:** dos

bacon (BAY-kun)

Spanish: tocino   **Pilipino:** tusino

Vietnamese: thịt lưng heo   **Chinese:** 熏肉 / 培根

Hmong: nqaij sawb   **French:** lard

badge (baj)

Spanish: insignia   **Pilipino:** tsapa

Vietnamese: huy hiệu   **Chinese:** 徽章

Hmong: daim ntawv coj qhia npe   **French:** insigne

baker (BAY-kur)

Spanish: panadera   **Pilipino:** panadero

Vietnamese: người nướng bánh   **Chinese:** 面包师 / 烤麵包師

Hmong: tus neeg ci qhaub cib thiab khoj noom   **French:** boulanger

a b c d e f g h i j k l m n o p q r s t u v w x y z

A
B
C
D
E
F
G
H
I
J
K
L
M
N
O
P
Q
R
S
T
U
V
W
X
Y
Z

ball (bahl)

Spanish: bola, pelota   **Pilipino:** bola

Vietnamese: trái banh   **Chinese:** 球

Hmong: lub pob, lub npas   **French:** balle

balloon (buh-LOON)

Spanish: globo   **Pilipino:** lobo

Vietnamese: bong bóng   **Chinese:** 汽球

Hmong: zais   **French:** ballon

ballplayer (BAHL-play-ur)

Spanish: jugador de pelota   **Pilipino:** manlalaro ng bola

Vietnamese: cầu thủ   **Chinese:** 球员／球員

Hmong: tus neeg ntaus pob   **French:** joueur de base-ball

banana (buh-NAN-uh)

Spanish: plátano   **Pilipino:** saging

Vietnamese: trái chuối   **Chinese:** 香蕉

Hmong: txiv tsawb   **French:** banane

bank teller (bangk TEL-ur)

Spanish: cajera   **Pilipino:** teler

Vietnamese: thư ký ngân hàng   **Chinese:** 银行出纳员／銀行出納員

Hmong: tus pauv nyiaj   **French:** caissier

barber (BAR-bur)

Spanish: peluquero, barbero

Pilipino: mangugupit

Vietnamese: thợ hớt tóc

Chinese: 理发师／理髮師

Hmong: kws txiav plaub hau

French: barbier, coitteur

barn (barn)

Spanish: granero

Pilipino: kamalig

Vietnamese: chuồng ngựa, chuồng trâu bò

Chinese: 谷仓／穀倉

Hmong: lub txhab

French: grange

bars (barz)

Spanish: barras

Pilipino: baras

Vietnamese: xà kép

Chinese: 杠杆／槓桿

Hmong: kav hlau

French: barres

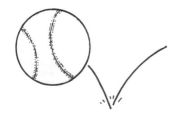

baseball (BAYS-bahl)

Spanish: béisbol

Pilipino: baseball

Vietnamese: dã cầu

Chinese: 棒球

Hmong: lub npas cuam

French: base-ball

bat (bat)

Spanish: bate

Pilipino: talibatab

Vietnamese: cái gậy

Chinese: 球棒

Hmong: qws ntaus npas

French: batte

a
b
c
d
e
f
g
h
i
j
k
l
m
n
o
p
q
r
s
t
u
v
w
x
y
z

ABCDEFGHIJKLMNOPQRSTUVWXYZ

bat (bat)

Spanish: murciélago **Pilipino:** paniki

Vietnamese: con dơi **Chinese:** 蝙蝠

Hmong: puav **French:** chauve-souris

bathing suit (BAY-thing soot)

Spanish: traje de baño **Pilipino:** damit panligo

Vietnamese: đồ tắm **Chinese:** 游泳衣

Hmong: khaub ncaws da dej **French:** maillot de bain

bathroom (BATH-room)

Spanish: cuarto de baño **Pilipino:** banyo, paliguan

Vietnamese: phòng tắm **Chinese:** 浴室

Hmong: chav dej **French:** salle de bains

bathtub (BATH-tub)

Spanish: bañera **Pilipino:** banyera

Vietnamese: bồn tắm **Chinese:** 浴缸

Hmong: dab da dej **French:** baignoire

bean (been)

Spanish: haba, frijol **Pilipino:** bins

Vietnamese: đậu **Chinese:** 豆

Hmong: taum **French:** haricot

Sounds Like Fun!

Think of three things that start with the /b/ sound that you like to play with. Ask a partner to guess what the things are.

bear (bayr)

Spanish: oso

Vietnamese: con gấu

Hmong: dais

Pilipino: oso

Chinese: 熊

French: ours

beaver (BEE-vur)

Spanish: castor

Vietnamese: con hải ly

Hmong: beaver

Pilipino: castor

Chinese: 海狸

French: castor

bed (bed)

Spanish: cama

Vietnamese: cái giường

Hmong: txaj

Pilipino: kama

Chinese: 床

French: lit

bedroom (BED-room)

Spanish: dormitorio

Vietnamese: phòng ngủ

Hmong: chav pw

Pilipino: silid-tulugan

Chinese: 寢室 / 寝室

French: chambre à coucher

bee (bee)

Spanish: abeja

Vietnamese: con ong

Hmong: muv

Pilipino: bubuyog

Chinese: 蜜蜂

French: abeille

a
b
c
d
e
f
g
h
i
j
k
l
m
n
o
p
q
r
s
t
u
v
w
x
y
z

A
B
C
D
E
F
G
H
I
J
K
L
M
N
O
P
Q
R
S
T
U
V
W
X
Y
Z

belt (belt)

Spanish: cinturón

Vietnamese: dây nịt

Hmong: txoj siv tawv

Pilipino: sinturon

Chinese: 皮带 / 皮帶

French: ceinture

bench (bench)

Spanish: banco, banca

Vietnamese: ghế dài

Hmong: lub rooj zaum

Pilipino: bangko

Chinese: 板凳

French: banc

bicycle (BY-sik-ul)

Spanish: bicicleta

Vietnamese: xe đạp

Hmong: nees zab, luv thim

Pilipino: bisikleta

Chinese: 脚踏车 / 腳踏車

French: bicyclette

bird (burd)

Spanish: pájaro

Vietnamese: con chim

Hmong: noog

Pilipino: ibon

Chinese: 鸟 / 鳥

French: oiseau

birthday (BURTH-day)

Spanish: cumpleaños

Vietnamese: sinh nhật

Hmong: hnub yug

Pilipino: kaarawan

Chinese: 生日

French: anniversaire

black (blak)

Spanish: negro

Vietnamese: màu đen

Hmong: dub

Pilipino: itim

Chinese: 黑

French: noir

block (blahk)

Spanish: cubo

Vietnamese: khối gỗ

Hmong: block

Pilipino: bloke

Chinese: 积木 / 積木

French: bloc

blouse (blous)

Spanish: blusa

Vietnamese: áo choàng

Hmong: tsho poj niam

Pilipino: blusa

Chinese: 上衫 / 上衣

French: corsage, chemisier

blue (bloo)

Spanish: azul

Vietnamese: màu xanh

Hmong: xiav

Pilipino: asul

Chinese: 蓝 / 藍

French: bleu

body (BAHD-ee)

Spanish: cuerpo

Vietnamese: cơ thể

Hmong: lub cev

Pilipino: katawan

Chinese: 身体 / 身體

French: corps

book (buk)

Spanish: libro

Vietnamese: cuốn sách

Hmong: phau ntawv

Pilipino: aklat

Chinese: 书 / 書

French: livre

boot (boot)

Spanish: bota

Vietnamese: giày ống

Hmong: khau tawv

Pilipino: botas

Chinese: 靴

French: botte

bow and arrow (boh and AYR-oh)

Spanish: arco y flecha

Vietnamese: cung và tên

Hmong: hneev nti thiab xib xub

Pilipino: panalaso at pana

Chinese: 弓 和 箭

French: arc et flèche

bowl (bohl)

Spanish: tazón

Vietnamese: cái chén

Hmong: tais

Pilipino: mangkok

Chinese: 碗

French: bol

boxer (BAHK-sur)

Spanish: boxeador

Vietnamese: người đấu quyền anh

Hmong: tus neeg ntaus nrig

Pilipino: boksingero

Chinese: 拳师 / 拳師

French: boxeur

boy (boy)

Spanish: muchacho   **Pilipino:** batang lalaki

Vietnamese: bé trai   **Chinese:** 男孩

Hmong: tus tub   **French:** garçon

bracelet (BRAYS-lit)

Spanish: pulsera   **Pilipino:** pulseras

Vietnamese: vòng   **Chinese:** 手镯

Hmong: saw tes   **French:** bracelet

bread (bred)

Spanish: pan   **Pilipino:** tinapay

Vietnamese: bánh mì   **Chinese:** 面包 / 麵包

Hmong: qhaub cib   **French:** pain

breakfast (BREK-fust)

Spanish: desayuno   **Pilipino:** almusal

Vietnamese: bữa ăn sáng   **Chinese:** 早餐

Hmong: tshais   **French:** petit déjeuner

bridge (brij)

Spanish: puente   **Pilipino:** tulay

Vietnamese: cây cầu   **Chinese:** 桥 / 橋

Hmong: choj   **French:** pont

a b c d e f g h i j k l m n o p q r s t u v w x y z

Dictionary Detective

Brown is a color. Find two other "b" words in this book that are colors.

broom (broom)

Spanish: escoba

Vietnamese: cái chổi

Hmong: khaub ruab

Pilipino: walis

Chinese: 扫帚 / 掃帚

French: balai

brother (BRUH-thur)

Spanish: hermano

Vietnamese: anh, em

Hmong: tij laug, kws, nus

Pilipino: kapatid na lalaki

Chinese: 兄弟

French: frère

brown (broun)

Spanish: marrón, café

Vietnamese: màu nâu

Hmong: xim kas fes

Pilipino: kayumanggi

Chinese: 褐色

French: marron

brush (brush)

Spanish: cepillo

Vietnamese: bàn chải

Hmong: khaub ruab

Pilipino: eskoba

Chinese: 刷

French: brosse

bucket (BUK-it)

Spanish: cubo, balde

Vietnamese: cái xô

Hmong: thoob

Pilipino: timba

Chinese: 桶

French: seau

buffalo (BUF-uh-loh)

Spanish: búfalo

Vietnamese: con bò rừng

Hmong: nyuj qus

Pilipino: tamaraw

Chinese: 水牛

French: buffle

bug (bug)

Spanish: insecto

Vietnamese: con rêp

Hmong: kab

Pilipino: kulisap

Chinese: 虫／蟲

French: punaise

bulletin board (BUL-uh-tun bord)

Spanish: tablón de anuncios

Vietnamese: bản thông báo

Hmong: daim ntoo lo ntawv

Pilipino: tabla ng bulitin

Chinese: 布告牌／公告欄

French: tableau d'affichage

bus (bus)

Spanish: autobús

Vietnamese: xe buýt

Hmong: npav

Pilipino: bus

Chinese: 公车／公車

French: autobus

bus driver (bus DRY-vur)

Spanish: conductora del autobús

Vietnamese: tài xế xe buýt

Hmong: tus tsav npav

Pilipino: tsuper ng bus

Chinese: 公车司机／公車司機

French: conducteur d'autobus

a
b
c
d
e
f
g
h
i
j
k
l
m
n
o
p
q
r
s
t
u
v
w
x
y
z

bush (boosh)

Spanish: arbusto   **Pilipino:** halaman

Vietnamese: bụi cây   **Chinese:** 灌木

Hmong: nroj tsuag   **French:** buisson

butcher (BOOCH-ur)

Spanish: carnicero   **Pilipino:** mangangatay

Vietnamese: người hàng thịt   **Chinese:** 肉販 / 肉販

Hmong: tus neeg tua tsiaj thiab   **French:** boucher
muag nqaij

butter (BUT-ur)

Spanish: mantequilla   **Pilipino:** mantikilya

Vietnamese: bơ   **Chinese:** 黄油 / 奶油

Hmong: butter   **French:** beurre

butterfly (BUT-ur-fly)

Spanish: mariposa   **Pilipino:** mariposa

Vietnamese: con bướm   **Chinese:** 蝴蝶

Hmong: npooj npaim   **French:** papillon

A B **B** C D E F G H I J K L M N O P Q R S T U V W X Y Z

Cc

a b **c** d e f g h i j k l m n o p q r s t u v w x y z

cafeteria
(kaf-uh-TEER-ee-uh)

Spanish: cafetería

Vietnamese: quán ăn tự dọn

Hmong: chaw noj mov

Pilipino: kapeteriya

Chinese: 自助餐馆 / 自助餐館

French: cafétéria

cake (kayk)

Spanish: pastel

Vietnamese: bánh ngọt

Hmong: khej, ncuav qab zib

Pilipino: keyk

Chinese: 蛋糕

French: gâteau

calendar (KAL-un-dur)

Spanish: calendario

Vietnamese: lịch

Hmong: ntawv saib hnub nyoos

Pilipino: kalendaryo

Chinese: 历 / 曆

French: calendrier

calf (kaf)

Spanish: becerro

Vietnamese: con bê

Hmong: me nyuam nyuj

Pilipino: bulo

Chinese: 小牛

French: veau

camel (KAM-ul)

Spanish: camello

Vietnamese: con lạc đà

Hmong: camel

Pilipino: kamelyo

Chinese: 骆驼 / 駱駝

French: chameau

camper (KAM-pur)

Spanish: vehículo para acampar

Vietnamese: xe cắm trại

Hmong: lub tsev txawb saum tsheb

Pilipino: kotse ng magkampamento

Chinese: 露营车 / 露營車

French: camping-car

can opener (kan OH-pun-ur)

Spanish: abrelatas

Vietnamese: cái khui đồ hộp

Hmong: tus tho kaus poom

Pilipino: abrelata

Chinese: 罐头启子 / 開罐器

French: ouvre-boîte

canoe (kuh-NOO)

Spanish: canoa

Vietnamese: thuyền

Hmong: nkoj txeeb kab

Pilipino: banka

Chinese: 独木舟 / 獨木舟

French: canoë

car (kar)

Spanish: coche

Vietnamese: xe

Hmong: tsheb

Pilipino: kotse

Chinese: 车 / 車

French: voiture

carpenter (KAR-pun-tur)

Spanish: carpintero

Vietnamese: người thợ

Hmong: neeg ua tsev

Pilipino: karpintero

Chinese: 木匠

French: charpentier

A B **C** D E F G H I J K L M N O P Q R S T U V W X Y Z

Sounds Like Fun!

Change the first letter in the word *cat* to make a new word. Make more new words just by changing the first letter. How many new words did you make?

carrot (KAYR-ut)

Spanish: zanahoria | **Pilipino:** karot

Vietnamese: củ cà rốt | **Chinese:** 葫萝卜 / 胡蘿蔔

Hmong: carrot | **French:** carotte

cat (kat)

Spanish: gato | **Pilipino:** pusa

Vietnamese: con mèo | **Chinese:** 猫 / 貓

Hmong: miv | **French:** chat

caterpillar (KAT-ur-pil-ur)

Spanish: oruga | **Pilipino:** higad

Vietnamese: con sâu | **Chinese:** 毛虫 / 毛毛蟲

Hmong: kab nyuam dev | **French:** chenille

CD (see-DEE)

Spanish: CD | **Pilipino:** CD

Vietnamese: đĩa CD | **Chinese:** 光盘 / 光碟

Hmong: CD | **French:** CD

CD player
(see-DEE PLAY-ur)

Spanish: lector de CD | **Pilipino:** CD player

Vietnamese: máy CD | **Chinese:** 光盘播放机 / 光碟播放機

Hmong: lub tso CD | **French:** lecteur de CD

a b c d e f g h i j k l m n o p q r s t u v w x y z

23

A
B
C
D
E
F
G
H
I
J
K
L
M
N
O
P
Q
R
S
T
U
V
W
X
Y
Z

ceiling (SEEL-ing)

Spanish: techo **Pilipino:** kisame

Vietnamese: trần nhà **Chinese:** 天花板

Hmong: ceiling **French:** plafond

celery (SEL-ree)

Spanish: apio **Pilipino:** sahud

Vietnamese: cần tây **Chinese:** 芹菜

Hmong: celery **French:** céleri

cement mixer
(suh-MENT MIK-sur)

Spanish: mezclador del cemento **Pilipino:** panghalo ng semento

Vietnamese: máy trộn hồ **Chinese:** 水泥搅拌器／水泥攪拌器

Hmong: lub cav tov xis mas **French:** bétonnière

cereal (SEER-ee-ul)

Spanish: cereal **Pilipino:** seryal

Vietnamese: ngũ cốc **Chinese:** 麦片粥／麥片粥

Hmong: khoj noom ntse mis **French:** céréale

chair (chayr)

Spanish: silla **Pilipino:** silya

Vietnamese: cái ghế **Chinese:** 椅子

Hmong: rooj zaum **French:** chaise

chalk (chahk)

Spanish: tiza

Vietnamese: phấn

Hmong: mem av

Pilipino: tsok

Chinese: 粉笔 / 粉筆

French: craie

chalkboard
(CHAHK-bord)

Spanish: pizarra

Vietnamese: bảng đen

Hmong: daim kas das

Pilipino: pisara

Chinese: 黑板

French: tableau

change (chaynj)

Spanish: cambio

Vietnamese: đồng tiền

Hmong: nyiaj lub, nyiaj xees seen

Pilipino: barya

Chinese: 零钱 / 零錢

French: monnaie

check (chek)

Spanish: cheque

Vietnamese: sự đình chi

Hmong: tshev

Pilipino: tseke

Chinese: 支票

French: chèque

checker (CHEK-ur)

Spanish: cajera

Vietnamese: người giữ két

Hmong: tus luj nqe

Pilipino: tseker

Chinese: 收银员 / 收銀員

French: caissière

a
b
c
d
e
f
g
h
i
j
k
l
m
n
o
p
q
r
s
t
u
v
w
x
y
z

25

A B **C** D E F G H I J K L M N O P Q R S T U V W X Y Z

cheek (cheek)

Spanish: mejilla

Pilipino: pisngi

Vietnamese: cái má

Chinese: 颊 / 頰

Hmong: plhu

French: joue

cheese (cheez)

Spanish: queso

Pilipino: keso

Vietnamese: phó mát

Chinese: 奶酪

Hmong: cheese

French: fromage

chemist (KEM-ist)

Spanish: química

Pilipino: kimiko

Vietnamese: nhà hoá học

Chinese: 化学家 / 化學家

Hmong: tus tov tshuaj

French: chimiste

cherry (CHAYR-ee)

Spanish: cereza

Pilipino: seresa

Vietnamese: anh đào

Chinese: 樱桃 / 櫻桃

Hmong: cherry

French: cerise

chest of drawers
(chest uv drorz)

Spanish: cómoda

Pilipino: kaha

Vietnamese: tủ có ngăn kéo

Chinese: (带抽屉的)衣橱 / 帶抽屉的衣橱

Hmong: tub rau khaub ncaws

French: commode

Sounds Like Fun!

Take "ch" away from *chin*. Then put each of the letters of the alphabet in front of "_in." Did you make any real words? What were they?

chick (chik)

Spanish: polluelo

Vietnamese: con gà con

Hmong: me nyuam qaib

Pilipino: sisiw

Chinese: 小鸡 / 小雞

French: poussin

chicken (CHIK-un)

Spanish: pollo

Vietnamese: con gà

Hmong: qiab

Pilipino: manok

Chinese: 鸡 / 雞

French: poulet

child (chyld)

Spanish: niño

Vietnamese: trẻ em

Hmong: me nyuam

Pilipino: bata

Chinese: 小孩

French: enfant

chimney (CHIM-nee)

Spanish: chimenea

Vietnamese: ống khói

Hmong: chimney

Pilipino: tsiminea

Chinese: 烟囱 / 煙囪

French: cheminée

chin (chin)

Spanish: barbilla, mentón

Vietnamese: cái cằm

Hmong: pob tsaig

Pilipino: baba

Chinese: 下巴

French: menton

a b c d e f g h i j k l m n o p q r s t u v w x y z

chipmunk (CHIP-munk)

Spanish: ardilla listada

Pilipino: ardilya sa lupa

Vietnamese: con sóc chuột

Chinese: 花栗鼠

Hmong: nas ciav

French: tamia

circle (SUR-kul)

Spanish: círculo

Pilipino: bilog

Vietnamese: vòng tròn

Chinese: 圆／圓

Hmong: vajvoog

French: cercle

city (SIT-ee)

Spanish: ciudad

Pilipino: siyudad

Vietnamese: thành phố

Chinese: 都市

Hmong: lub zos

French: ville

clock (klahk)

Spanish: reloj

Pilipino: orasan

Vietnamese: đồng hồ

Chinese: 钟／鐘

Hmong: lub moos

French: horloge

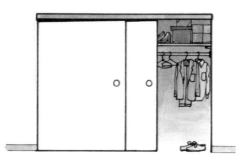

closet (KLAHZ-it)

Spanish: armario, ropero

Pilipino: kloset

Vietnamese: cái tủ

Chinese: 壁橱

Hmong: kem tsev rau khoom

French: placard

clothesline (KLOHZ-lyn)

Spanish: cuerda para tender la ropa

Pilipino: sampayan

Vietnamese: dây phơi quần áo

Chinese: 晒衣绳 / 曬衣繩

Hmong: hlua ziab khaub ncaws

French: corde à linge

clothespin (KLOHZ-pin)

Spanish: pinza para tender ropa

Pilipino: sipit

Vietnamese: kẹp phơi quần áo

Chinese: 衣服夹 / 衣服夾

Hmong: pas tais khaub ncaws

French: pince à linge

clown (kloun)

Spanish: payaso

Pilipino: payaso

Vietnamese: tên hề

Chinese: 小丑

Hmong: clown

French: clown

coat (koht)

Spanish: chaqueta

Pilipino: balok

Vietnamese: áo ngoài

Chinese: 外套

Hmong: tsho tiv no

French: manteau

coffee maker
(KAHF-ee MAY-kur)

Spanish: máquina de café

Pilipino: gawaan ng kape

Vietnamese: máy pha cà phê

Chinese: 咖啡器

Hmong: lub ua kas fes

French: cafetière électrique

A B **C** D E F G H I J K L M N O P Q R S T U V W X Y Z

coffeepot (KAHF-ee-paht)

Spanish: cafetera

Pilipino: lutuan ng kape

Vietnamese: bình cà phê

Chinese: 咖啡壶 / 咖啡壺

Hmong: lub rhaub kas fes

French: cafetière

colt (kohlt)

Spanish: potro

Pilipino: batang kabayo

Vietnamese: ngựa đực con

Chinese: 小马 / 小馬

Hmong: me nyuam nees

French: poulain

comb (kohm)

Spanish: peine

Pilipino: suklay

Vietnamese: cái lược

Chinese: 梳子

Hmong: zuag

French: peigne

computer (kum-PYOO-tur)

Spanish: computadora

Pilipino: komputer

Vietnamese: máy điện toán

Chinese: 电子计算机 / 電腦

Hmong: computer

French: ordinateur

cook (kuk)

Spanish: cocinero

Pilipino: kusinero, tagapagluto

Vietnamese: người đầu bếp

Chinese: 厨师 / 厨師

Hmong: tus ua zaub mov

French: cuisinier

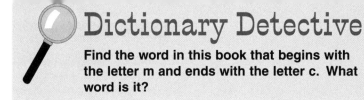

Dictionary Detective

Find the word in this book that begins with the letter m and ends with the letter c. What word is it?

cookie (KUK-ee)

Spanish: galleta

Pilipino: kuki

Vietnamese: bánh

Chinese: 饼乾 / 餅乾

Hmong: khoj noom

French: biscuit

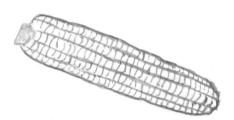

corn (korn)

Spanish: maíz, elote

Pilipino: mais

Vietnamese: bắp

Chinese: 玉蜀黍

Hmong: pob kws

French: maïs

cottage cheese (KAHT-ij cheez)

Spanish: requesón

Pilipino: keso

Vietnamese: phó mát trắng

Chinese: 农家奶酪 / 農家奶酪

Hmong: cottage cheese

French: fromage blanc

cousin (KUZ-in)

Spanish: primo

Pilipino: pinsan

Vietnamese: người anh em họ

Chinese: 堂兄,弟,姊,妹

Hmong: kwv tij

French: cousin

cow (kou)

Spanish: vaca

Pilipino: baka

Vietnamese: con bò

Chinese: 奶牛

Hmong: nyuj

French: vache

a b c d e f g h i j k l m n o p q r s t u v w x y z

A
B
C
D
E
F
G
H
I
J
K
L
M
N
O
P
Q
R
S
T
U
V
W
X
Y
Z

cowboy (KOU-boy)

Spanish: vaquero   **Pilipino:** kawboy

Vietnamese: ông chăn bò   **Chinese:** 牛仔

Hmong: tub zov nyuj   **French:** cowboy

cowgirl (KOU-gurl)

Spanish: vaquera   **Pilipino:** kawgirl

Vietnamese: cô gái chăn bò   **Chinese:** 女牛仔

Hmong: ntxhais zov nyuj   **French:** cowgirl

coyote (ky-OHT-ee)

Spanish: coyote   **Pilipino:** koyote

Vietnamese: sói đồng cỏ   **Chinese:** 小狼,山狗

Hmong: hma   **French:** coyote

cracker (KRAK-ur)

Spanish: galleta   **Pilipino:** kraker

Vietnamese: bánh bích quy dòn   **Chinese:** 硬饼乾 / 鹹餅乾

Hmong: khoj noom   **French:** cracker

crane (krayn)

Spanish: grúa   **Pilipino:** derik

Vietnamese: máy trục   **Chinese:** 起重机 / 起重機

Hmong: crane   **French:** grue

crayon (KRAY-on)

Spanish: lápiz de cera **Pilipino:** krayola

Vietnamese: viết chì màu **Chinese:** 蜡笔 / 蠟筆

Hmong: xim **French:** crayon de couleur

crib (krib)

Spanish: cuna **Pilipino:** kuna

Vietnamese: giường giữ em bé **Chinese:** 婴儿床 / 嬰兒床

Hmong: lub txoj rau me nyuam mos pw **French:** lit d'enfant

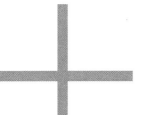

cross (krahs)

Spanish: cruz **Pilipino:** krus

Vietnamese: dấu chữ thập **Chinese:** 十字形

Hmong: khaub lig **French:** croix

cup and saucer (kup and SAH-sur)

Spanish: taza y platillo **Pilipino:** tasa at platito

Vietnamese: tách và đĩa **Chinese:** 杯子和茶碟

Hmong: khob thiab phaj **French:** tasse et soucoupe

cupcake (KUP-kayk)

Spanish: pastelito en molde **Pilipino:** kapkeyk

Vietnamese: bánh nướng hình tách **Chinese:** 杯形饼 / 杯形餅

Hmong: cupcake **French:** petit gâteau

A
B
C
D
E
F
G
H
I
J
K
L
M
N
O
P
Q
R
S
T
U
V
W
X
Y
Z

curve (kurv)

Spanish: curva

Pilipino: kurba

Vietnamese: đường cong

Chinese: 弯 / 彎

Hmong: nkhaus

French: courbe

custodian
(kus-TOH-dee-un)

Spanish: guardián

Pilipino: diyanitor

Vietnamese: người trông coi

Chinese: 清洁工 / 清潔工

Hmong: tus tu tsev

French: gardien

dancer (DANS-ur)

Spanish: bailarina   **Pilipino:** mananayaw

Vietnamese: vũ công   **Chinese:** 舞蹈家

Hmong: tus neeg seev cev   **French:** danseur

December (dee-SEM-bur)

Spanish: diciembre   **Pilipino:** Disyembre

Vietnamese: Tháng Chạp,   **Chinese:** 十二月
Tháng Mười Hai

Hmong: lub kaum ob hlis   **French:** décembre

deer (deer)

Spanish: ciervo, venado   **Pilipino:** usa

Vietnamese: con nai   **Chinese:** 鹿

Hmong: mos lwj   **French:** cerf

den (den)

Spanish: estudio   **Pilipino:** den

Vietnamese: phòng riêng nhỏ   **Chinese:** 小房

Hmong: ib hoob nyob los sis   **French:** petit salon
saib ntawv

dentist (DEN-tist)

Spanish: dentista   **Pilipino:** dentista

Vietnamese: nha sĩ   **Chinese:** 牙医 / 牙醫

Hmong: kws kho hniav   **French:** dentiste

a b c **d** e f g h i j k l m n o p q r s t u v w x y z

35

A
B
C
D
E
F
G
H
I
J
K
L
M
N
O
P
Q
R
S
T
U
V
W
X
Y
Z

Dictionary Detective

The guide words on this page are *desk* and *dining room*. What page number has the guide words *hat* and *helicopter*?

desk (desk)

Spanish: escritorio **Pilipino:** desk

Vietnamese: cái bàn **Chinese:** 桌子

Hmong: rooj sau ntawv **French:** bureau

diamond (DY-mund)

Spanish: diamante **Pilipino:** diamante

Vietnamese: hình thoi **Chinese:** 钻石 / 鑽石

Hmong: diamond **French:** losange

diaper (DY-pur)

Spanish: pañal **Pilipino:** lampin

Vietnamese: tả lót **Chinese:** 尿布

Hmong: daiv pawm **French:** couche

dime (dym)

Spanish: moneda de diez centavos **Pilipino:** sampung pera

Vietnamese: đồng mười xu **Chinese:** 一角

Hmong: kaum xees **French:** pièce de 10 cents

dining room (DYN-ing room)

Spanish: comedor **Pilipino:** silid kainan

Vietnamese: phòng ăn **Chinese:** 饭厅 / 飯廳

Hmong: chav noj mov **French:** salle à manger

dinner (DIN-ur)

Spanish: cena
Pilipino: hapunan

Vietnamese: bữa ăn tối
Chinese: 晚餐

Hmong: hmo
French: dîner

dinosaur (DY-nuh-sor)

Spanish: dinosaurio
Pilipino: dinosaur

Vietnamese: con khủng long
Chinese: 恐龙 / 恐龍

Hmong: dinosaur
French: dinosaure

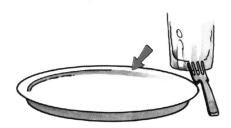

dish (dish)

Spanish: plato
Pilipino: pinggan, plato

Vietnamese: cái dĩa
Chinese: 盘子 / 盤子

Hmong: tais diav
French: plat

dishpan (DISH-pan)

Spanish: barreño de fregar platos
Pilipino: hugasan ng pinggan

Vietnamese: bồn rửa chén dĩa
Chinese: 洗碟用盆子 / 洗碗槽

Hmong: lub tais rau tais diav
French: bassine

diskette (dihz-KET)

Spanish: disco, disquete flexible
Pilipino: diskett

Vietnamese: dĩa từ
Chinese: 磁盘, 磁碟 / 磁碟片

Hmong: diskette
French: disquette

A B C D E F G H I J K L M N O P Q R S T U V W X Y Z

doctor (DAHK-tur)

Spanish: médica

Pilipino: doktor

Vietnamese: bác sĩ

Chinese: 医师／醫師

Hmong: kws kho mob

French: docteur

dog (dahg)

Spanish: perro

Pilipino: aso

Vietnamese: con chó

Chinese: 狗

Hmong: aub, dev

French: chien

doll (dahl)

Spanish: muñeca

Pilipino: manyika

Vietnamese: búp bê

Chinese: 玩偶

Hmong: me nyuam roj hmab

French: poupée

dollar bill (DAHL-ur bil)

Spanish: dólar

Pilipino: isang dolyar

Vietnamese: tờ giấy bạc

Chinese: 一元纸钞／一元紙鈔

Hmong: nyiaj duas las

French: billet d'un dollar

dollhouse (DAHL-hous)

Spanish: casa de muñecas

Pilipino: bahay bahayan

Vietnamese: nhà búp bê

Chinese: 玩偶屋

Hmong: tsev ua si rau me nyam roj hmab

French: maison de poupée

dolphin (DAHL-fin)

Spanish: delfín **Pilipino:** dolpin

Vietnamese: cá heo **Chinese:** 海豚

Hmong: dolphin **French:** dauphin

door (dor)

Spanish: puerta **Pilipino:** pintuan

Vietnamese: cánh cửa **Chinese:** 门 / 門

Hmong: qhov rooj **French:** porte

dot (daht)

Spanish: punto **Pilipino:** tuldok

Vietnamese: dấu chấm **Chinese:** 点 / 點

Hmong: ib tee **French:** point

doughnut (DOH-nut)

Spanish: dona **Pilipino:** donat

Vietnamese: bánh ngọt **Chinese:** 面包圈 / 甜甜圈

Hmong: doughnut **French:** beignet

dress (dres)

Spanish: vestido **Pilipino:** bestida

Vietnamese: áo đầm **Chinese:** 洋装 / 洋裝

Hmong: tiab txuas tsho **French:** robe

a
b
c
d
e
f
g
h
i
j
k
l
m
n
o
p
q
r
s
t
u
v
w
x
y
z

A B C D E F G H I J K L M N O P Q R S T U V W X Y Z

dressmaker
(DRES-may-kur)

Spanish: costurera

Vietnamese: thợ may áo quần phụ nữ

Hmong: tus neeg xaw tiab

Pilipino: mananahe

Chinese: 女裝裁縫师 / 女裝裁縫師

French: couturière

drinking fountain
(DRINK-ing FOUN-tun)

Spanish: fuente de agua potable

Vietnamese: vòi nước uống

Hmong: tus kais haus dej

Pilipino: inominang bukal

Chinese: 饮水器 / 飲水機

French: fontaine d'eau potable

drum (drum)

Spanish: tambor

Vietnamese: cái trống

Hmong: nruas

Pilipino: tambol

Chinese: 鼓

French: tambour

duck (duk)

Spanish: pato

Vietnamese: con vịt

Hmong: os

Pilipino: pato

Chinese: 鸭 / 鴨

French: canard

dustpan (DUST-pan)

Spanish: recogedor

Vietnamese: cái hốt rác

Hmong: cib laug

Pilipino: pandakot, pansaluk dumi

Chinese: 簸箕 / 畚箕

French: pelle à poussière

eagle (EE-gul)

Spanish: águila

Pilipino: agila

Vietnamese: con chim ó

Chinese: 鷹／鷹

Hmong: dav

French: aigle

ear (eer)

Spanish: oreja

Pilipino: tainga

Vietnamese: cái tai

Chinese: 耳

Hmong: pob ntseg

French: oreille

egg (eg)

Spanish: huevo

Pilipino: itlog

Vietnamese: cái trứng

Chinese: 蛋

Hmong: qe

French: oeuf

eight (ayt)

8

eight pennies

Spanish: ocho

Pilipino: walo

Vietnamese: tám

Chinese: 八

Hmong: yim

French: huit

eighteen (ay-TEEN)

18

eighteen snails

Spanish: dieciocho

Pilipino: labingwalo

Vietnamese: mười tám

Chinese: 十八

Hmong: kaum yim

French: dix-huit

eighth (ayth)

Spanish: octavo

Pilipino: pangwalo

Vietnamese: thứ tám

Chinese: 第八

Hmong: thib yim

French: huitième

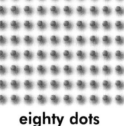
80

eighty dots

eighty (AY-tee)

Spanish: ochenta

Pilipino: walumpu

Vietnamese: tám mươi

Chinese: 八十

Hmong: yim caum

French: quatre-vingts

elbow (EL-boh)

Spanish: codo

Pilipino: siko

Vietnamese: cái khủy tay

Chinese: 肘

Hmong: luj tshib

French: coude

electrician (ih-lek-TRISH-un)

Spanish: electricista

Pilipino: elektrisista

Vietnamese: thợ điện

Chinese: 电气技师 / 電氣技師

Hmong: tus kho hluav taws xob

French: électricien

elephant (EL-uh-funt)

Spanish: elefante

Pilipino: elepante

Vietnamese: con voi

Chinese: 象

Hmong: ntxhw

French: éléphant

A B C D E F G H I J K L M N O P Q R S T U V W X Y Z

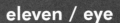
Sounds Like Fun!

Read aloud the "e" words on this page and clap as you say each syllable. How many words have only one syllable? How many have two? How many have three?

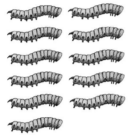

11

eleven caterpillars

eleven (EE-lev-un)

Spanish: once

Pilipino: labing-isa

Vietnamese: mười một

Chinese: 十一

Hmong: kaum ib

French: onze

e-mail (EE-mayl)

Spanish: correo electrónico

Pilipino: e-mail

Vietnamese: thư điện tử

Chinese: 电子邮件 / 電子郵件

Hmong: e-mail

French: courrier électronique

engineer (en-juh-NEER)

Spanish: ingeniero

Pilipino: inhinyero

Vietnamese: kỹ sư

Chinese: 工程师 / 工程師

Hmong: engineer

French: ingénieur

eraser (ee-RAY-sur)

Spanish: borrador

Pilipino: pambura

Vietnamese: cục tẩy

Chinese: 橡皮

Hmong: lub lwv ntawv

French: gomme

eye (I)

Spanish: ojo

Pilipino: mata

Vietnamese: con mắt

Chinese: 眼

Hmong: qhov muag

French: œil

a b c d e f g h i j k l m n o p q r s t u v w x y z

43

eyebrow (I-brou)

Spanish: ceja

Pilipino: kilay

Vietnamese: lông mày

Chinese: 眉毛

Hmong: plaub muag theem saum toj

French: sourcil

eyelash (I-lash)

Spanish: pestaña

Pilipino: pilik mata

Vietnamese: lông mi

Chinese: 睫毛

Hmong: pluab muag

French: cil

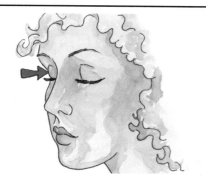

eyelid (I-lid)

Spanish: párpado

Pilipino: takup mata

Vietnamese: mí mắt

Chinese: 眼皮

Hmong: tawv muag

French: paupière

face (fays)

Spanish: cara

Pilipino: mukha

Vietnamese: cái mặt

Chinese: 脸 / 臉

Hmong: ntsej muag

French: visage

fall (fahl)

Spanish: otoño

Pilipino: taglagas

Vietnamese: mùa thu

Chinese: 秋

Hmong: lub caij nplooj ntoos zeeg

French: automne

family (FAM-lee)

Spanish: familia

Pilipino: pamilya

Vietnamese: gia đình

Chinese: 家族

Hmong: tsev neeg

French: famille

family room
(FAM-lee room)

Spanish: cuarto de estar

Pilipino: silid pamilya

Vietnamese: phòng gia đình

Chinese: 起居室

Hmong: chav tsev neeg nyob

French: salle de séjour

fan (fan)

Spanish: ventilador

Pilipino: bentilador

Vietnamese: cái quạt

Chinese: 电风扇 / 電風扇

Hmong: kiv cua

French: ventilateur

a b c d e f g h i j k l m n o p q r s t u v w x y z

farmer (FAR-mur)

Spanish: granjero

Pilipino: magsasaka

Vietnamese: nông gia

Chinese: 农夫／農夫

Hmong: tswv teb, neeg ua liag ua teb

French: fermier

father (FAH-thur)

Spanish: padre

Pilipino: ama

Vietnamese: cha

Chinese: 父亲／父親

Hmong: txiv

French: père

fawn (fahn)

Spanish: cervato

Pilipino: batang usa

Vietnamese: con hươu con

Chinese: 小鹿

Hmong: me nyuam mos lwj

French: faon

February (FEB-yoo-ayr-ee)

Spanish: febrero

Pilipino: Pebrero

Vietnamese: Tháng Hai

Chinese: 二月

Hmong: lub ob hlis

French: février

15

fifteen (fif-TEEN)

fifteen ladybugs

Spanish: quince

Pilipino: labinlima

Vietnamese: mười lăm

Chinese: 十五

Hmong: kaum tsib

French: quinze

A B C D E F G H I J K L M N O P Q R S T U V W X Y Z

fifth (fifth)

Spanish: quinto

Pilipino: panlima

Vietnamese: thứ năm

Chinese: 第五

Hmong: thib tsib

French: cinquième

fifty (FIF-tee)

50

fifty dots

Spanish: cincuenta

Pilipino: limampu

Vietnamese: năm mươi

Chinese: 五十

Hmong: tsib caug

French: cinquante

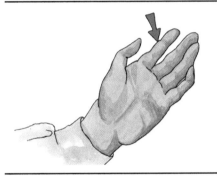

finger (FING-ur)

Spanish: dedo

Pilipino: daliri

Vietnamese: ngón tay

Chinese: 手指

Hmong: ntiv tes

French: doigt

fingernail
(FING-ur-nayl)

Spanish: uña

Pilipino: kuko

Vietnamese: móng tay

Chinese: 指甲

Hmong: rau tes

French: ongle

fire engine (fyr EN-jun)

Spanish: coche de bomberos

Pilipino: trak ng bombero

Vietnamese: xe cứu hỏa

Chinese: 消防车／消防車

Hmong: tsheb tua hluav taws

French: voiture de pompiers

a
b
c
d
e
f
g
h
i
j
k
l
m
n
o
p
q
r
s
t
u
v
w
x
y
z

Dictionary Detective

Find the first "w" word in this book. What word is it?

A B C D E **F** G H I J K L M N O P Q R S T U V W X Y Z

firefighter (FYR-fyt-ur)

Spanish: bombero   **Pilipino:** bombero

Vietnamese: lính cứu hỏa **Chinese:** 消防员 / 消防員

Hmong: neeg tua hluav taws **French:** pompier

first (furst)

Spanish: primero   **Pilipino:** una

Vietnamese: thứ nhứt   **Chinese:** 第一

Hmong: thib ib   **French:** premier

fish (fish)

Spanish: pez   **Pilipino:** isda

Vietnamese: con cá   **Chinese:** 鱼 / 魚

Hmong: ntses   **French:** poisson

5

five blocks

five (fyv)

Spanish: cinco   **Pilipino:** lima

Vietnamese: năm   **Chinese:** 五

Hmong: tsib   **French:** cinq

flag (flag)

Spanish: bandera   **Pilipino:** watawat

Vietnamese: lá cờ   **Chinese:** 旗

Hmong: chij   **French:** drapeau

floor (flor)

Spanish: piso

Pilipino: sahig

Vietnamese: sàn nhà

Chinese: 地板

Hmong: lub plag tsev

French: sol

flower (FLOU-ur)

Spanish: flor

Pilipino: bulaklak

Vietnamese: bông hoa

Chinese: 花

Hmong: lub paj

French: fleur

fly (fly)

Spanish: mosca

Pilipino: langaw

Vietnamese: con ruồi

Chinese: 苍蝇 / 蒼蠅

Hmong: yoov

French: mouche

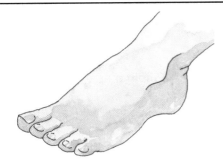

foot (fut)

Spanish: pie

Pilipino: paa

Vietnamese: cái bàn chân

Chinese: 脚 / 腳

Hmong: taw

French: pied

football (FUT-bahl)

Spanish: pelota de fútbol

Pilipino: putbol

Vietnamese: túc cầu

Chinese: 足球

Hmong: football

French: ballon de football américain

A B C D E F G H I J K L M N O P Q R S T U V W X Y Z

forehead (FOR-hed)

Spanish: frente

Vietnamese: cái trán

Hmong: hauv pliaj

Pilipino: noo

Chinese: 额 / 額頭

French: front

fork (fork)

Spanish: tenedor

Vietnamese: cái nĩa

Hmong: diav rawg

Pilipino: tinidor

Chinese: 叉

French: fourchette

40
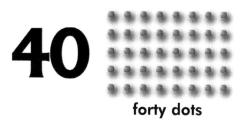
forty dots

forty (FOR-tee)

Spanish: cuarenta

Vietnamese: bốn mươi

Hmong: plaub caug

Pilipino: apatnapu

Chinese: 四十

French: quarante

4

four balloons

four (for)

Spanish: cuatro

Vietnamese: bốn

Hmong: plaub

Pilipino: apat

Chinese: 四

French: quatre

14

fourteen spiders

fourteen (for-TEEN)

Spanish: catorce

Vietnamese: mười bốn

Hmong: kaum plaub

Pilipino: labing-apat

Chinese: 十四

French: quatorze

fourth (forth)

Spanish: cuarto

Pilipino: pangapat

Vietnamese: thứ tư

Chinese: 第四

Hmong: thib plaub

French: quatrième

fox (fahks)

Spanish: zorro

Pilipino: soro

Vietnamese: con chồn

Chinese: 狐

Hmong: hma

French: renard

Friday (FRY-day)

Spanish: viernes

Pilipino: Biyernes

Vietnamese: Thứ Sáu

Chinese: 星期五

Hmong: Friday

French: vendredi

frog (frahg)

Spanish: rana

Pilipino: palaka

Vietnamese: con ếch

Chinese: 青蛙

Hmong: qav

French: grenouille

frying pan (FRY-ing pan)

Spanish: sartén

Pilipino: kawali

Vietnamese: cái chảo

Chinese: 炒锅 / 炒鍋

Hmong: lub yias

French: poêle

a b c d e f g h i j k l m n o p q r s t u v w x y z

Gg

A B C D E F **G** H I J K L M N O P Q R S T U V W X Y Z

game (gaym)

Spanish: juego

Vietnamese: trò chơi

Hmong: kev ua si

Pilipino: laro

Chinese: 游戏 / 遊戲

French: jeu

gardener (GARD-nur)

Spanish: jardinero

Vietnamese: người làm vườn

Hmong: neej tus vaj

Pilipino: hardinero

Chinese: 园丁 / 園丁

French: jardinier

giraffe (juh-RAF)

Spanish: jirafa

Vietnamese: hươu cao cổ

Hmong: nees caj dab ntev

Pilipino: hirapa

Chinese: 长颈鹿 / 長頸鹿

French: girafe

girl (gurl)

Spanish: muchacha

Vietnamese: con gái

Hmong: tus ntxhais

Pilipino: batang babae

Chinese: 女孩

French: fille

glass (glas)

Spanish: vaso

Vietnamese: cái ly

Hmong: khob iav

Pilipino: baso

Chinese: 玻璃

French: verre

glasses (GLAS-iz)

Spanish: gafas, anteojos, lentes   **Pilipino:** salamin sa mata

Vietnamese: kính đeo mắt   **Chinese:** 眼镜 / 眼鏡

Hmong: lub tsom qhov muag   **French:** lunettes

globe (glohb)

Spanish: globo terráqueo   **Pilipino:** globo

Vietnamese: quả địa cầu   **Chinese:** 地球仪 / 地球儀

Hmong: lub ntiaj teb   **French:** globe

glove (gluv)

Spanish: guante   **Pilipino:** guwantes

Vietnamese: găng tay   **Chinese:** 手套

Hmong: hnab looj tes   **French:** gant

glue (gloo)

Spanish: pegamento   **Pilipino:** pandikit

Vietnamese: keo dán   **Chinese:** 胶 / 膠

Hmong: kua nplaum   **French:** colle

goat (goht)

Spanish: cabra   **Pilipino:** kambing

Vietnamese: con dê   **Chinese:** 山羊

Hmong: tus tshis   **French:** chèvre

Sounds Like Fun!
Complete this sentence with a "g" word: "The girl gave her grandmother a ___." Now ask some friends to finish the sentence with other "g" words.

goose (goos)

Spanish: ganso
Pilipino: gansa
Vietnamese: con ngỗng
Chinese: 鵝 / 鵝
Hmong: os quab
French: oie

gorilla (guh-RIL-uh)

Spanish: gorila
Pilipino: gurilya
Vietnamese: con khỉ đột
Chinese: 大猩猩
Hmong: ib hom liab
French: gorille

grandfather (GRAND-fah-thur)

Spanish: abuelo
Pilipino: ingkong, lolo
Vietnamese: ông nội, ông ngoại
Chinese: 祖父
Hmong: yawg
French: grand-père

grandmother (GRAND-muh-thur)

Spanish: abuela
Pilipino: impo, lola
Vietnamese: bà nội, bà ngoại
Chinese: 祖母
Hmong: pog
French: grand-mère

grape (grayp)

Spanish: uva
Pilipino: ubas
Vietnamese: trái nho
Chinese: 葡萄
Hmong: grape
French: raisin

A B C D E F G H I J K L M N O P Q R S T U V W X Y Z

54

grapefruit (GRAYP-froot)

Spanish: pomelo, toronja

Pilipino: suha

Vietnamese: trái bưởi

Chinese: 柚子

Hmong: txiv lws zoov

French: pamplemousse

grass (gras)

Spanish: hierba, césped

Pilipino: damo

Vietnamese: cỏ

Chinese: 草

Hmong: nyom

French: herbe

grasshopper (GRAS-hahp-ur)

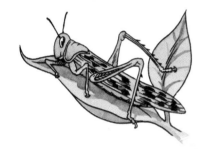

Spanish: saltamontes

Pilipino: tipaklong

Vietnamese: con châu chấu

Chinese: 蚱蜢

Hmong: kooj txig

French: sauterelle

green (green)

Spanish: verde

Pilipino: berde

Vietnamese: màu xanh lá cây

Chinese: 绿 / 綠

Hmong: ntsuab

French: vert

guitar (gih-TAR)

Spanish: guitarra

Pilipino: gitara

Vietnamese: lục huyền cầm

Chinese: 吉他

Hmong: kiv taj, teev tee

French: guitare

gum (gum)

Spanish: goma de mascar, chicle

Vietnamese: nướu răng, kẹo cao su

Hmong: khoj noom yas

Pilipino: gum

Chinese: 橡皮糖 / 口香糖

French: gomme à mâcher, chewing gum

hair (hayr)

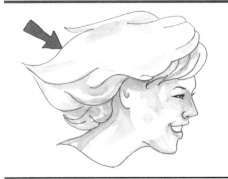

Spanish: pelo

Vietnamese: tóc

Hmong: plaub hau

Pilipino: buhok

Chinese: 头发 / 頭髮

French: cheveux

hairbrush (HAYR-brush)

Spanish: cepillo para el pelo

Vietnamese: bàn chải tóc

Hmong: zuag ntsis plaubhau

Pilipino: eskoba ng buhok

Chinese: 发刷 / 髮刷

French: brosse à chevaux

hairdresser (HAYR-dres-ur)

Spanish: peinadora

Vietnamese: thợ cắt tóc

Hmong: tus kho plaubhau

Pilipino: tagapagkulot

Chinese: 美发师 / 美髮師

French: coiffeur

half-dollar (haf-DAHL-ur)

Spanish: medio dólar

Vietnamese: nửa mỹ kim

Hmong: lub nyiaj tsib caug xees

Pilipino: kalahati ng dolyar

Chinese: 半块钱 / 半塊錢

French: pièce de cinquante cents

half-hour (haf-OUR)

Spanish: media hora

Vietnamese: nửa giờ

Hmong: peb caug nas this

Pilipino: kalahating oras

Chinese: 半小时 / 半小時

French: demi-heure

a b c d e f g **h** i j k l m n o p q r s t u v w x y z

half past (haf past)

half past 2 o'clock

Spanish: dos y media

Pilipino: ... i media

Vietnamese: nửa giờ sau

Chinese: 过了半··· / 過了牛···

Hmong: peb caug nas this dhau

French: et demi

ham (ham)

Spanish: jamón

Pilipino: hamon

Vietnamese: thịt heo

Chinese: 火腿

Hmong: ib hom nqaij

French: jambon

hamburger
(HAM-bur-gur)

Spanish: hamburguesa

Pilipino: hamburger

Vietnamese: bánh mì mềm kẹp thịt bằm

Chinese: 煎牛肉饼 / 漢堡

Hmong: hamburger

French: hamburger

hammer (HAM-ur)

Spanish: martillo

Pilipino: martilyo

Vietnamese: cái búa

Chinese: 锤 / 鎚

Hmong: rauj

French: marteau

hand (hand)

Spanish: mano

Pilipino: kamay

Vietnamese: bàn tay

Chinese: 手

Hmong: tes

French: main

hat (hat)

Spanish: sombrero   **Pilipino:** sumbrero

Vietnamese: cái mũ   **Chinese:** 帽子

Hmong: kos mom   **French:** chapeau

head (hed)

Spanish: cabeza   **Pilipino:** ulo

Vietnamese: cái đầu   **Chinese:** 头 / 頭

Hmong: taub hau   **French:** tête

heater (HEET-ur)

Spanish: calentador   **Pilipino:** panginit

Vietnamese: lò sưởi   **Chinese:** 暖气 / 暖氣機

Hmong: lub tso pa sov   **French:** appareil de chauffage

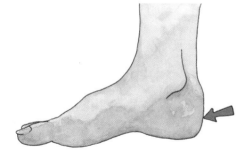

heel (heel)

Spanish: talón   **Pilipino:** sakong

Vietnamese: gót chân   **Chinese:** 后脚跟 / 後脚跟

Hmong: pob taws   **French:** talon

helicopter (HEL-ih-kahp-tur)

Spanish: helicóptero   **Pilipino:** helikopter

Vietnamese: máy bay trực thăng   **Chinese:** 直升飞机 / 直昇飛機

Hmong: nyuj hoom qav taub   **French:** hélicoptère

a b c d e f g **h** i j k l m n o p q r s t u v w x y z

Dictionary Detective

Hen and *horse* are animals. What is the only word in this book that is an animal which begins with the letter z?

hen (hen)

Spanish: gallina

Pilipino: inahin

Vietnamese: con gà mái

Chinese: 母鸡 / 母雞

Hmong: poj qaib

French: poule

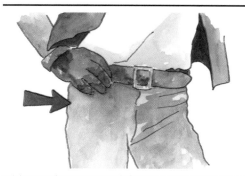

hip (hip)

Spanish: cadera

Pilipino: balakang

Vietnamese: cái hông

Chinese: 臀部

Hmong: ntshag

French: hanche

hippopotamus
(hip-uh-PAHT-uh-mus)

Spanish: hipopótamo

Pilipino: hipopotamus

Vietnamese: con hà mã

Chinese: 河马 / 河馬

Hmong: npua dej

French: hippopotame

hoe (hoh)

Spanish: azada, azadón

Pilipino: asarol

Vietnamese: cái cuốc

Chinese: 镐 / 鈀

Hmong: hlau

French: binette, pioche, bêche

horse (hors)

Spanish: caballo

Pilipino: kabayo

Vietnamese: con ngựa

Chinese: 马 / 馬

Hmong: nees

French: cheval

hose (hohz)

Spanish: manguera

Vietnamese: ống nước

Hmong: hlua dej, xaim dej

Pilipino: gomang pandilig

Chinese: 水管

French: tuyau

hot dog (HAHT dahg)

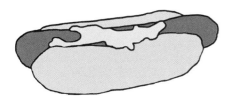

Spanish: perro caliente

Vietnamese: xúc xích

Hmong: nyuv txwm

Pilipino: hotdog

Chinese: 热狗 / 熱狗

French: hot-dog

hour (our)

Spanish: hora

Vietnamese: giờ đồng hồ

Hmong: xuam moos

Pilipino: oras

Chinese: 小时 / 小時

French: heure

hour hand (our hand)

hour
hand

Spanish: manilla de reloj

Vietnamese: kim chỉ giờ

Hmong: tus tes qhia xuam moos

Pilipino: maikling kamay ng relo

Chinese: 时针 / 時針

French: petite aiguille

a
b
c
d
e
f
g
h
i
j
k
l
m
n
o
p
q
r
s
t
u
v
w
x
y
z

ice cream (iz kreem)

Spanish: helado

Pilipino: sorbetes

Vietnamese: cà rem

Chinese: 冰淇淋

Hmong: kee lees

French: glace

ice skate (iz skayt)

Spanish: patín del hielo

Pilipino: isket sa yelo

Vietnamese: giày trượt băng

Chinese: 滑冰 / 滑冰

Hmong: ice skate

French: patin à glace

Internet (IN-tur-net)

Spanish: Internet

Pilipino: Internet

Vietnamese: liên mạng

Chinese: 国际互联网 / 網際網路

Hmong: eevthawsnem

French: Internet

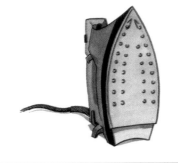

iron (I-urn)

Spanish: plancha

Pilipino: plantsa

Vietnamese: cái bàn ủi

Chinese: 熨斗

Hmong: lus luam khaub ncaws

French: fer à repasser

ironing board (I-urn-ing bord)

Spanish: mesa de planchar

Pilipino: plantsahan

Vietnamese: bàn có lót nệm để ủi

Chinese: 熨衣板

Hmong: daim txiag luam khaub ncaws

French: planche à repasser, table à repasser

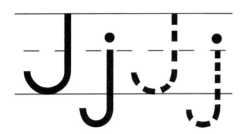

jacket (JAK-it)

Spanish: chaqueta

Pilipino: diyaket

Vietnamese: áo khoát ngoài

Chinese: 夹克 / 夾克

Hmong: tsho tiv no

French: veste

jam (jam)

Spanish: mermelada

Pilipino: halaya

Vietnamese: mứt

Chinese: 果酱 / 果醬

Hmong: jam

French: confiture

January (JAN-yoo-ayr-ee)

Spanish: enero

Pilipino: Enero

Vietnamese: Tháng Giêng

Chinese: 一月

Hmong: ib hlis

French: janvier

jaw (jah)

Spanish: quijada

Pilipino: panga

Vietnamese: cái hàm

Chinese: 颚 / 顎

Hmong: puab tsaig

French: mâchoire

jeep (jeep)

Spanish: jeep

Pilipino: dyip

Vietnamese: xe gíp

Chinese: 吉普车 / 吉普車

Hmong: tsheb, jeep

French: jeep

a
b
c
d
e
f
g
h
i
j
k
l
m
n
o
p
q
r
s
t
u
v
w
x
y
z

jello (JEL-oh)

Spanish: gelatina   **Pilipino:** gulaman

Vietnamese: món thạch đông   **Chinese:** 果冻 / 果凍

Hmong: jello   **French:** am gelée

jelly (JEL-ee)

Spanish: jalea, mermelada   **Pilipino:** halaya

Vietnamese: thạch đông   **Chinese:** 果酱 / 果醬

Hmong: ntsiavlim   **French:** gelée

jet (jet)

Spanish: avión de reacción   **Pilipino:** dyet

Vietnamese: phản lực cơ   **Chinese:** 喷射机 / 噴射機

Hmong: davhlau   **French:** avion à réaction

judge (juj)

Spanish: juez   **Pilipino:** hukom

Vietnamese: thẩm phán   **Chinese:** 法官

Hmong: tus txiav txim   **French:** juge

juice (joos)

Spanish: jugo   **Pilipino:** katas

Vietnamese: nước trái cây   **Chinese:** 果汁

Hmong: kua txiv ntoo   **French:** jus

A B C D E F G H I J K L M N O P Q R S T U V W X Y Z

Dictionary Detective

Jump rope is made of two words: *jump* and *rope*. Find five other words that are made of two words. What are they?

July (juh-LY)

Spanish: julio

Pilipino: Hulyo

Vietnamese: Tháng Bảy

Chinese: 七月

Hmong: xya hlis

French: juillet

jump rope (jump rohp)

Spanish: saltador, cuerda de saltar

Pilipino: talon lubid

Vietnamese: dây để nhảy

Chinese: 跳绳 / 跳繩

Hmong: txoj hlua dhia

French: corde à sauter

June (joon)

Spanish: junio

Pilipino: Hunyo

Vietnamese: Tháng Sáu

Chinese: 六月

Hmong: rau hlis

French: juin

a b c d e f g h i j k l m n o p q r s t u v w x y z

kangaroo
(kang-guh-ROO)

Spanish: canguro

Vietnamese: con đại thử

Hmong: kangaroo

Pilipino: kanggaro

Chinese: 袋鼠

French: kangourou

key (kee)

Spanish: llave

Vietnamese: chìa khóa

Hmong: yawm sij, kas ces

Pilipino: susi

Chinese: 钥匙 / 鑰匙

French: clef

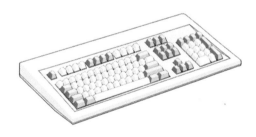

keyboard (KEE-bord)

Spanish: teclado

Vietnamese: bàn phím chữ

Hmong: keyboard

Pilipino: teklado

Chinese: 键盘 / 鍵盤

French: clavier

king (king)

Spanish: rey

Vietnamese: ông vua

Hmong: huab tais

Pilipino: hari

Chinese: 国王 / 國王

French: roi

kitchen (KICH-un)

Spanish: cocina

Vietnamese: nhà bếp

Hmong: chav ua noj

Pilipino: kusina

Chinese: 厨房 / 廚房

French: cuisine

kite (kyt)

Spanish: cometa

Pilipino: saranggola

Vietnamese: con diều

Chinese: 鸢,风筝 / 風箏

Hmong: lub khaij

French: cerf-volant

kitten (KIT-un)

Spanish: gatito

Pilipino: kuting

Vietnamese: con mèo con

Chinese: 小猫 / 小貓

Hmong: me nyuam miv

French: chaton

knee (nee)

Spanish: rodilla

Pilipino: tuhod

Vietnamese: đầu gối

Chinese: 膝盖 / 膝蓋

Hmong: hauv caug

French: genou

knife (nyf)

Spanish: cuchillo

Pilipino: lanseta

Vietnamese: con dao

Chinese: 刀

Hmong: riam

French: couteau

a b c d e f g h i j **k** l m n o p q r s t u v w x y z

A B C D E F G H I J K L M N O P Q R S T U V W X Y Z

ladder (LAD-ur)

Spanish: escalera

Pilipino: hagdan

Vietnamese: cái thang

Chinese: 梯子

Hmong: ntaiv

French: échelle

ladybug (LAYD-ee-bug)

Spanish: mariquita

Pilipino: kulisap

Vietnamese: con bọ hung

Chinese: 瓢虫 / 瓢蟲

Hmong: kab huab txhib

French: coccinelle

lake (layk)

Spanish: lago

Pilipino: lawa

Vietnamese: cái hồ

Chinese: 湖

Hmong: lub pas dej

French: lac

lamb (lam)

Spanish: cordero

Pilipino: kordero

Vietnamese: con cừu non

Chinese: 小羊

Hmong: me nyuam yaj

French: agneau

lamp (lamp)

Spanish: lámpara

Pilipino: ilawan

Vietnamese: cái đèn

Chinese: 灯 / 檯燈

Hmong: lub teeb

French: lampe

Sounds Like Fun!

Think of three things that start with the /l/ sound. Ask a partner to guess what they are.

leg (leg)

Spanish: pierna

Pilipino: pata

Vietnamese: cái chân

Chinese: 腿

Hmong: txhais ceg

French: jambe

lemon (LEM-un)

Spanish: limón

Pilipino: limon

Vietnamese: trái chanh

Chinese: 柠檬 / 檸檬

Hmong: mas naus

French: citron

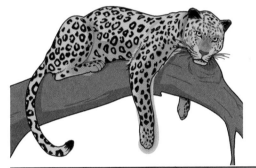

leopard (LEP-urd)

Spanish: leopardo

Pilipino: leopard

Vietnamese: con báo

Chinese: 豹

Hmong: tsov txaij

French: léopard

letter (LET-ur)

Spanish: carta

Pilipino: liham

Vietnamese: lá thư

Chinese: 书信 / 書信

Hmong: tsab ntawv

French: lettre

lettuce (LET-us)

Spanish: lechuga

Pilipino: litsugas

Vietnamese: rau diếp

Chinese: 萵苣

Hmong: zaub qhwv

French: laitue

a b c d e f g h i j k **l** m n o p q r s t u v w x y z

A B C D E F G H I J K **L** M N O P Q R S T U V W X Y Z

librarian
(ly-BRAYR-ee-un)

Spanish: bibliotecaria
Vietnamese: quản thủ thư viện
Hmong: tus saib tsev nyeem ntawv

Pilipino: laybraryan
Chinese: 图书馆员 / 圖書館員
French: bibliothécaire

library (LY-brayr-ee)

Spanish: biblioteca
Vietnamese: thư viện
Hmong: tsev nyeem ntawv

Pilipino: aklatan
Chinese: 图书馆 / 圖書館
French: bibliothèque

lifeguard (LYF-gard)

Spanish: salvavidas
Vietnamese: người cứu đắm
Hmong: tus saib kom txob muaj neeg poob deg

Pilipino: tagapagligtas
Chinese: 救生员 / 救生員
French: maître nageur

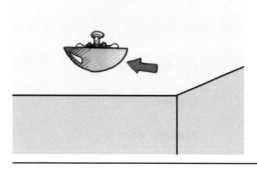

light (lyt)

Spanish: luz
Vietnamese: ánh sáng, đèn
Hmong: teeb

Pilipino: ilaw
Chinese: 灯光 / 燈光
French: lumière

line (lyn)

Spanish: línea
Vietnamese: đường
Hmong: txoj kab

Pilipino: linya
Chinese: 线 / 線
French: ligne

lion (LY-un)

Spanish: león **Pilipino:** leon

Vietnamese: con sư tử **Chinese:** 狮子 / 獅子

Hmong: tso ntxhuav **French:** lion

lip (lip)

Spanish: labio **Pilipino:** labi

Vietnamese: môi **Chinese:** 唇

Hmong: de ncauj **French:** lèvre

living room (LIV-ing room)

Spanish: sala de estar **Pilipino:** salas

Vietnamese: phòng khách **Chinese:** 起居室

Hmong: chav nyob **French:** salle

lizard (LIZ-urd)

Spanish: lagarto **Pilipino:** lagarto

Vietnamese: con rắn mối **Chinese:** 蜥蜴

Hmong: nab qa **French:** lézard

lobster (LAHB-stur)

Spanish: langosta **Pilipino:** ulang

Vietnamese: con tôm hùm **Chinese:** 龙虾 / 龍蝦

Hmong: cws **French:** homard

a
b
c
d
e
f
g
h
i
j
k
l
m
n
o
p
q
r
s
t
u
v
w
x
y
z

A
B
C
D
E
F
G
H
I
J
K
L
M
N
O
P
Q
R
S
T
U
V
W
X
Y
Z

lock (lahk)

Spanish: candado, cerradura

Pilipino: kandado

Vietnamese: ổ khóa

Chinese: 锁 / 鎖

Hmong: ntsuas poo

French: cadenas

lunch (lunch)

Spanish: almuerzo

Pilipino: tanghalian

Vietnamese: bữa ăn trưa

Chinese: 午餐

Hmong: su

French: déjeuner

Mm Mm

magazine
(MAG-uh-zeen)

Spanish: revista

Vietnamese: tạp chí

Hmong: magazine

Pilipino: magasin

Chinese: 杂志 / 雜誌

French: magazine

mail carrier
(mayl KAYR-ee-ur)

Spanish: cartera

Vietnamese: người phát thư

Hmong: tus neeg nqa ntawv

Pilipino: kartero

Chinese: 邮递员 / 郵遞員

French: facteur

mail truck (mayl truk)

Spanish: carro del correo

Vietnamese: xe thư

Hmong: lub tsheb xa ntawv

Pilipino: trak ng koreo

Chinese: 邮递开车 / 郵遞卡車

French: fourgonnette des postes

man (man)

Spanish: hombre

Vietnamese: người đàn ông

Hmong: txiv neej

Pilipino: lalaki

Chinese: 男子

French: homme

map (map)

Spanish: mapa

Vietnamese: bản đồ

Hmong: pheem thib

Pilipino: mapa

Chinese: 地图 / 地圖

French: carte

a b c d e f g h i j k l **m** n o p q r s t u v w x y z

Dictionary Detective

Find the only word in this book that begins with the letter i and ends with the letter m. What word is it?

March (march)

Spanish: marzo

Pilipino: Marso

Vietnamese: Tháng Ba

Chinese: 三月

Hmong: peb hlis ntuj

French: mars

May (may)

Spanish: mayo

Pilipino: Mayo

Vietnamese: Tháng Năm

Chinese: 五月

Hmong: tsib hlis ntuj

French: mai

meat (meet)

Spanish: carne

Pilipino: karne

Vietnamese: thịt

Chinese: 肉

Hmong: nqaij

French: viande

mechanic (muh-KAN-ik)

Spanish: mecánico

Pilipino: mekaniko

Vietnamese: thợ máy

Chinese: 机械工 / 機械工

Hmong: tus khos tsheb

French: mécanicien

microwave oven (MY-kroh-wayv UV-un)

Spanish: microonda

Pilipino: microwave oven

Vietnamese: lò vi ba

Chinese: 微波炉 / 微波爐

Hmong: qhov cub hluav taws xob

French: four à micro-ondes

milk (milk)

Spanish: leche   **Pilipino:** gatas

Vietnamese: sữa   **Chinese:** 牛奶

Hmong: mis nyuj   **French:** lait

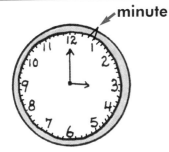

minute

minute (MIN-it)

Spanish: minuto   **Pilipino:** minuto

Vietnamese: phút   **Chinese:** 分

Hmong: nas thi   **French:** minute

minute hand

minute hand (MIN-it hand)

Spanish: minutero   **Pilipino:** mahabang kamay ng relo

Vietnamese: kim chỉ phút   **Chinese:** 分针 / 分針

Hmong: tus tes qhia nas thi   **French:** grande aiguille

mirror (MEER-ur)

Spanish: espejo   **Pilipino:** salamin

Vietnamese: gương soi   **Chinese:** 镜 / 鏡

Hmong: daim iav   **French:** miroir

mitten (MIT-un)

Spanish: guante, mitón   **Pilipino:** guwantes

Vietnamese: găng hở ngón   **Chinese:** 手套

Hmong: hnab loog tes   **French:** mouffle

a b c d e f g h i j k l **m** n o p q r s t u v w x y z

75

moccasin
(MAHK-uh-sun)

Spanish: mocasín

Pilipino: mokasin

Vietnamese: giày da đế bẹt

Chinese: 平底鞋

Hmong: ib hom khau

French: mocassin

Monday (MUN-day)

Spanish: lunes

Pilipino: Lunes

Vietnamese: Thứ Hai

Chinese: 星期一

Hmong: Monday

French: lundi

monitor (MAHN-ih-tur)

Spanish: monitór

Pilipino: monitor

Vietnamese: máy quan sát

Chinese: 屏幕 / 電腦螢幕

Hmong: monitor

French: moniteur

monkey (MUN-kee)

Spanish: mono

Pilipino: unggoy

Vietnamese: con khỉ

Chinese: 猴

Hmong: tus liab

French: singe

moose (moos)

Spanish: alce

Pilipino: anta

Vietnamese: con một loài hươu

Chinese: 麋鹿

Hmong: moose

French: orignal

A B C D E F G H I J K L **M** N O P Q R S T U V W X Y Z

mop (mahp)

Spanish: trapeador, fregona **Pilipino:** panlampaso

Vietnamese: cây lau nhà **Chinese:** 拖把

Hmong: tus txhuam tsev **French:** serpillière

mosquito (muh-SKEET-oh)

Spanish: mosquito **Pilipino:** lamok

Vietnamese: con muỗi **Chinese:** 蚊

Hmong: yoov tshaj cum **French:** moustique

mother (MUH-thur)

Spanish: madre **Pilipino:** ina

Vietnamese: mẹ **Chinese:** 母亲 / 母親

Hmong: niam **French:** mère

motorcycle (MOH-tur-sy-kul)

Spanish: motocicleta **Pilipino:** motorsiklo

Vietnamese: xe gắn máy **Chinese:** 机器脚踏车 / 摩托車

Hmong: mau taus **French:** moto

mouse (mous)

Spanish: ratón **Pilipino:** daga

Vietnamese: con chuột **Chinese:** 鼠

Hmong: tus nas **French:** souris

a
b
c
d
e
f
g
h
i
j
k
l
m
n
o
p
q
r
s
t
u
v
w
x
y
z

A
B
C
D
E
F
G
H
I
J
K
L
M
N
O
P
Q
R
S
T
U
V
W
X
Y
Z

mouse (mous)

Spanish: ratón de computadora   **Pilipino:** mouse

Vietnamese: con chuột   **Chinese:** 鼠标器 / 鼠標器

Hmong: mouse   **French:** souris

mouth (mouth)

Spanish: boca   **Pilipino:** bibig

Vietnamese: cái miệng   **Chinese:** 嘴

Hmong: qhov ncauj   **French:** bouche

moving van (MOO-ving van)

Spanish: camión de mudanzas   **Pilipino:** trak ng paglipat

Vietnamese: xe van dọn nhà   **Chinese:** 搬家卡车 / 搬家卡車

Hmong: tsheb thauj khoom tsiv   **French:** camion de déménagement

musician (myoo-ZISH-un)

Spanish: músico   **Pilipino:** musikero

Vietnamese: nhạc sĩ   **Chinese:** 音乐家 / 音樂家

Hmong: neeg ntau nruas tshuab raj   **French:** musicien

Nn Nn

nail (nayl)

Spanish: clavo

Pilipino: pako

Vietnamese: cái đinh

Chinese: 钉子 / 釘子

Hmong: ntsia hlau

French: clou

napkin (NAP-kin)

Spanish: servilleta

Pilipino: serbilyeta

Vietnamese: khăn lau

Chinese: 餐巾

Hmong: ntawv thiab ntaub so ncauj

French: serviette

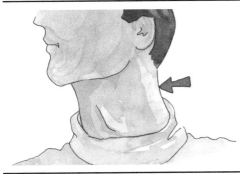

neck (nek)

Spanish: cuello

Pilipino: leeg

Vietnamese: cái cổ

Chinese: 颈 / 頸

Hmong: caj dab

French: cou

necklace (NEK-lis)

Spanish: collar

Pilipino: kuwintas

Vietnamese: dây chuyền

Chinese: 项链 / 項鍊

Hmong: saw caj dab

French: collier

news carrier (nooz KAYR-ee-ur)

Spanish: repartidor de periódicos

Pilipino: mensahero

Vietnamese: người phát báo

Chinese: 送报员 / 送報員

Hmong: tus xas ntawv

French: livreur de journaux

a b c d e f g h i j k l m **n** o p q r s t u v w x y z

79

Sounds Like Fun!

What number word do you see in *nineteen* and *ninety*? If you said, "nine," you are right. Think of other number words you can put in front of "___teen" and "___ty." What new words can you make?

newspaper (NOOZ-pay-pur)

Spanish: periódico, diario

Vietnamese: báo chí

Hmong: ntawv xov xum

Pilipino: diyaryo

Chinese: 报纸 / 報紙

French: journal

nickel (NIK-ul)

Spanish: moneda de cinco centavos

Vietnamese: đồng năm xu

Hmong: tsib xees

Pilipino: limang sentimos

Chinese: 五分钱 / 五分錢

French: pièce de cinq cents

nine (nyn)

9

nine bananas

Spanish: nueve

Vietnamese: chín

Hmong: cuaj

Pilipino: siyam

Chinese: 九

French: neuf

nineteen (nyn-TEEN)

19

nineteen cherries

Spanish: diecinueve

Vietnamese: mười chín

Hmong: kaum cuaj

Pilipino: labinsiyam

Chinese: 十九

French: dix-neuf

ninety (NYN-tee)

90

ninety dots

Spanish: noventa

Vietnamese: chín mươi

Hmong: cuaj caum

Pilipino: siyamnapu

Chinese: 九十

French: quatre-vingt-dix

ninth (nynth)

Spanish: noveno

Pilipino: ikasiyam

Vietnamese: thứ chín

Chinese: 第九

Hmong: thib cuaj

French: neuvième

nose (nohz)

Spanish: nariz

Pilipino: ilong

Vietnamese: cái mũi

Chinese: 鼻

Hmong: taub ntswm

French: nez

November (noh-VEM-bur)

Spanish: noviembre

Pilipino: Nobyembre

Vietnamese: Tháng Mười Một

Chinese: 十一月

Hmong: kaum ib hlis ntuj

French: novembre

nurse (nurs)

Spanish: enfermera

Pilipino: nars

Vietnamese: y tá

Chinese: 护士 / 護士

Hmong: nurse

French: infirmière

nut (nut)

Spanish: nuez

Pilipino: mane

Vietnamese: đậu phụng

Chinese: 坚果 / 堅果

Hmong: noob txiv ntoo

French: noix

a b c d e f g h i j k l m **n** o p q r s t u v w x y z

81

O o

ocean (OH-shun)

Spanish: océano   **Pilipino:** karagatan

Vietnamese: đại dương   **Chinese:** 海洋

Hmong: dej hiav txwv, dej ntuj   **French:** océan

October (ahk-TOH-bur)

Spanish: octubre   **Pilipino:** Oktubre

Vietnamese: Tháng Mười   **Chinese:** 十月

Hmong: kaum hli ntuj   **French:** octobre

octopus (AHK-tuh-pus)

Spanish: pulpo   **Pilipino:** oktopus

Vietnamese: con bạch tuộc   **Chinese:** 章鱼 / 章魚

Hmong: octopus   **French:** pieuvre

office (AHF-is)

Spanish: oficina   **Pilipino:** opisina

Vietnamese: văn phòng   **Chinese:** 办公室 / 辦公室

Hmong: chaw ua hauj lwm   **French:** bureau

one (wun)

1

one soccer ball

Spanish: uno   **Pilipino:** isa

Vietnamese: một   **Chinese:** 一

Hmong: ib   **French:** un

100

one hundred dots

one hundred
(wun HUN-dred)

Spanish: cien

Pilipino: isandaan

Vietnamese: một trăm

Chinese: 一百

Hmong: ib puas

French: cent

onion (UN-yen)

Spanish: cebolla

Pilipino: sibuyas

Vietnamese: củ hành

Chinese: 洋葱

Hmong: lub dos loj

French: oignon

orange (OR-inj)

Spanish: naranja

Pilipino: mamulamulang-dilaw

Vietnamese: màu cam

Chinese: 橘色

Hmong: xim liab ziv, tsiv tsuav

French: orange

orange (OR-inj)

Spanish: naranja

Pilipino: dalandan

Vietnamese: trái cam

Chinese: 橘 ／ 柳橙

Hmong: txiv kab ntxwv

French: orange

ostrich (AHS-trich)

Spanish: avestruz

Pilipino: ostrik

Vietnamese: con đà điểu

Chinese: 鸵鸟 ／ 鴕鳥

Hmong: ostrich

French: autruche

Sounds Like Fun!

Pick a word that begins with the letter o and draw a picture for each letter in the word. For example, for *owl*, you might draw an <u>o</u>nion, a <u>w</u>orm, and a <u>l</u>amp. Ask a friend to guess the word by looking at your picture.

oval (OH-vul)

Spanish: oval

Vietnamese: hình bầu dục

Hmong: oval

Pilipino: obalo

Chinese: 椭圆形 / 橢圓形

French: ovale

owl (oul)

Spanish: búho

Vietnamese: con cú

Hmong: tus plas

Pilipino: kuwago

Chinese: 猫头鹰 / 貓頭鷹

French: hibou

A B C D E F G H I J K L M N O P Q R S T U V W X Y Z

Pp

page (payj)

Spanish: página   **Pilipino:** pahina

Vietnamese: trang giấy   **Chinese:** 页 / 頁

Hmong: phab ntawv   **French:** page

pail (payl)

Spanish: cubo   **Pilipino:** timba

Vietnamese: cái xô   **Chinese:** 桶

Hmong: lub thoob   **French:** seau

painter (PAYNT-ur)

Spanish: pintor   **Pilipino:** pintor

Vietnamese: thợ sơn   **Chinese:** 油漆工

Hmong: tus pleev xim   **French:** peintre

pajamas (puh-JAH-muhz)

Spanish: pijamas   **Pilipino:** padyama

Vietnamese: áo quần ngủ   **Chinese:** 睡衣

Hmong: kob ncaws hnav pw   **French:** pyjamas

pan (pan)

Spanish: cacerola   **Pilipino:** kawali

Vietnamese: cái nồi   **Chinese:** 锅 / 鍋

Hmong: lauj kaub   **French:** casserole

a b c d e f g h i j k l m n o **p** q r s t u v w x y z

pancake (PAN-kayk)

Spanish: crepe, tortita, panqueque

Pilipino: pankeyk

Vietnamese: bánh kếp

Chinese: 薄烤饼／薄烤餅

Hmong: pancake

French: crêpe

pants (pants)

Spanish: pantalones

Pilipino: pantalon

Vietnamese: cái quần

Chinese: 裤／褲

Hmong: lub ris

French: pantalon

paper (PAY-pur)

Spanish: papel

Pilipino: papel

Vietnamese: giấy

Chinese: 纸／紙

Hmong: daim ntawv

French: papier

parrot (PAYR-ut)

Spanish: loro

Pilipino: loro

Vietnamese: con vẹt

Chinese: 鹦鹉／鸚鵡

Hmong: leeb nkaub

French: perroquet

paste (payst)

Spanish: engrudo

Pilipino: pandikit

Vietnamese: bột nhão

Chinese: 糊

Hmong: kua nplaum

French: pâte

patio (PAT-ee-oh)

Spanish: patio

Pilipino: patiyo

Vietnamese: hiên nhà

Chinese: 平台／陽台

Hmong: lawj (siab)

French: patio

pea (pee)

Spanish: guisante

Pilipino: gisantes

Vietnamese: đậu xanh

Chinese: 豌豆

Hmong: noob taum pauv

French: pois

peacock (PEE-kahk)

Spanish: pavo real

Pilipino: paboreal

Vietnamese: con công

Chinese: 孔雀

Hmong: noog yaj yuam

French: paon

peanut butter
(PEE-nut BUT-ur)

Spanish: manteca de cacahuete, manteca de maní

Pilipino: mantikilya ng mani

Vietnamese: bơ đậu phụng

Chinese: 花生酱／花生醬

Hmong: txiv laum huab zeeb zom

French: beurre de cacahuètes

pear (payr)

Spanish: pera

Pilipino: peras

Vietnamese: trái lê

Chinese: 梨子

Hmong: pear

French: poire

a b c d e f g h i j k l m n o **p** q r s t u v w x y z

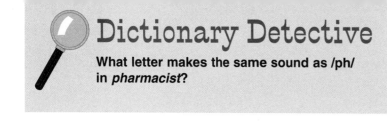

Dictionary Detective

What letter makes the same sound as /ph/ in *pharmacist*?

pencil (PEN-sul)

Spanish: lápiz

Pilipino: lapis

Vietnamese: bút chì

Chinese: 铅笔 / 鉛筆

Hmong: xom

French: crayon

pencil sharpener
(PEN-sul SHAR-puh-nur)

Spanish: sacapuntas de lápiz

Pilipino: pantasa

Vietnamese: máy bào bút chì

Chinese: 转笔刀 / 削鉛筆機

Hmong: lub hliav xom

French: taille-crayons

penguin (PENG-gwin)

Spanish: pingüino

Pilipino: pengguwin

Vietnamese: chim cánh ngắn

Chinese: 企鹅 / 企鵝

Hmong: penguin

French: pingouin, manchot

---

penny (PEN-ee)

Spanish: centavo

Pilipino: isang pera

Vietnamese: đồng xu

Chinese: 一分 / 一分錢

Hmong: lub ib xeev

French: pièce de 1 cent

pharmacist
(FAR-muh-sist)

Spanish: farmacéutico

Pilipino: parmaseutiko

Vietnamese: dược sĩ

Chinese: 药剂师 / 藥劑師

Hmong: tus kws tshuaj

French: pharmacien

A B C D E F G H I J K L M N O **P** Q R S T U V W X Y Z

88

piano (pee-AN-oh)

Spanish: piano

Pilipino: piyano

Vietnamese: dương cầm

Chinese: 钢琴 / 鋼琴

Hmong: piano

French: piano

pie (py)

Spanish: pastel

Pilipino: pay

Vietnamese: bánh ba tê

Chinese: 馅饼 / 餡餅

Hmong: lub phais

French: tarte

pig (pig)

Spanish: cerdo

Pilipino: baboy

Vietnamese: con heo

Chinese: 猪

Hmong: tus npua

French: porc

pilot (PY-lut)

Spanish: piloto

Pilipino: piloto

Vietnamese: phi công

Chinese: 飞机驾驶员 / 飛機駕駛員

Hmong: tus tsav dav hlau

French: pilote

piñata (pee-NYAH-tah)

Spanish: piñata

Pilipino: pinyata

Vietnamese: gói đồ chơi treo lên để đập bể dịp lễ

Chinese: 墨西哥生日玩具

Hmong: piñata

French: piñata

Left margin: A B C D E F G H I J K L M N O **P** Q R S T U V W X Y Z

pineapple (PYN-ap-ul)

Spanish: piña   **Pilipino:** pinya

Vietnamese: trái thơm   **Chinese:** 菠萝 / 鳳梨

Hmong: txiv puv luj   **French:** ananas

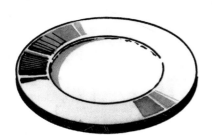

plate (playt)

Spanish: plato   **Pilipino:** plato

Vietnamese: cái đĩa   **Chinese:** 盘 / 盤

Hmong: phaj   **French:** assiette

playground (PLAY-ground)

Spanish: campo de juegos   **Pilipino:** palaruan

Vietnamese: sân chơi   **Chinese:** 游戏场地 / 遊戲場地

Hmong: chaw ua si   **French:** cour de jeu, cour de récréation

plumber (PLUM-ur)

Spanish: plomero, fontanero   **Pilipino:** plomero

Vietnamese: thợ ống nước   **Chinese:** 铅工 / 鉛工

Hmong: kws kho dej   **French:** plombier

polar bear (POH-lur bayr)

Spanish: oso polar   **Pilipino:** oso na galing sa mayelong lugar

Vietnamese: con gấu trắng   **Chinese:** 北极熊 / 北極熊

Hmong: dais dawb   **French:** ours blanc, ours polaire

police car
(puh-LEES kar)

Spanish: coche de policía

Vietnamese: xe cảnh sát

Hmong: tub ceev xwm tsheb

Pilipino: kotse ng pulis

Chinese: 警车 / 警車

French: voiture de police

police officer
(puh-LEES AH-fis-ur)

Spanish: agente de policía

Vietnamese: cảnh sát viên

Hmong: tus ceev xwm

Pilipino: opisyal ng pulis

Chinese: 警察

French: officier de police, policier

popcorn (PAHP-korn)

Spanish: palomitas

Vietnamese: bắp rang dòn

Hmong: paj kws

Pilipino: binusang mais

Chinese: 爆米花

French: pop-corn

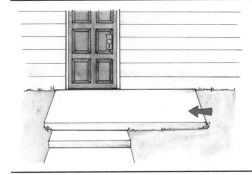

porch (porch)

Spanish: pórtico

Vietnamese: hiên nhà

Hmong: lawj (qis)

Pilipino: portiko

Chinese: 门口 / 門口

French: porche

porcupine
(POR-kyuh-pyn)

Spanish: puerco espín

Vietnamese: con nhím

Hmong: tsaug

Pilipino: porkoespin

Chinese: 豪猪

French: porc-épic

a b c d e f g h i j k l m n o **p** q r s t u v w x y z

A
B
C
D
E
F
G
H
I
J
K
L
M
N
O
P
Q
R
S
T
U
V
W
X
Y
Z

potato (puh-TAY-toh)

Spanish: patata, papa **Pilipino:** patatas

Vietnamese: khoai tây **Chinese:** 土豆 / 馬鈴薯

Hmong: qos yaj ywm **French:** pomme de terre

potato chip (puh-TAY-toh chip)

Spanish: papas fritas **Pilipino:** potato tsip

Vietnamese: lát khoai tây chiên dòn **Chinese:** 油炸土豆片 / 洋芋片

Hmong: potato chip **French:** chips

president (PREZ-uh-dunt)

Spanish: presidente **Pilipino:** pangulo

Vietnamese: tổng thống **Chinese:** 总统 / 總統

Hmong: tus nom **French:** président

principal (PRIN-suh-pul)

Spanish: directora **Pilipino:** punong-guro

Vietnamese: hiệu trưởng **Chinese:** 校长 / 校長

Hmong: tus thaw hauv tsev kawm ntawv **French:** principal

pumpkin (PUMP-kin)

Spanish: calabaza **Pilipino:** kalabasa

Vietnamese: bí ngô **Chinese:** 南瓜

Hmong: taub **French:** potiron

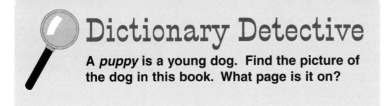

Dictionary Detective

A *puppy* is a young dog. Find the picture of the dog in this book. What page is it on?

puppy (PUP-ee)

Spanish: perrito

Pilipino: tuta

Vietnamese: con chó con

Chinese: 小狗

Hmong: me nyuam aub, me nyuam dev

French: chiot

purple (PUR-pul)

Spanish: morado, violeta

Pilipino: purpura

Vietnamese: màu tím

Chinese: 紫红色

Hmong: tsam xem

French: violet

purse (purs)

Spanish: monedero, bolsa

Pilipino: portamoneda

Vietnamese: cái bóp xách tay

Chinese: 钱包 / 錢包

Hmong: hnab nqa ntawm tes, kas paus

French: sac à main

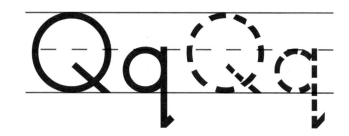

quarter (KWORT-ur)

Spanish: moneda de 25 centavos

Pilipino: ikaapat

Vietnamese: đồng hai mười lăm xu

Chinese: 二毛五

Hmong: lub nyiaj nees nkaum tsib xees

French: pièce de 25 cents

quarter past 8 o'clock

quarter past (KWORT-ur past)

Spanish: … y quarto

Pilipino: menos kinse

Vietnamese: quá mười lăm phút

Chinese: 过十五分 / 過十五分

Hmong: kaum tsib na thi dhau

French: et quart

quarter to 5 o'clock

quarter to (till) (KWORT-ur too [til])

Spanish: un cuarto para las…

Pilipino: para

Vietnamese: kém mười lăm phút (đến)

Chinese: 差十五分

Hmong: tshuav kaum tsib na thi

French: moins le quart

queen (kween)

Spanish: reina

Pilipino: reyna

Vietnamese: nữ hoàng

Chinese: 女王

Hmong: poj huab tais

French: reine

A B C D E F G H I J K L M N O P **Q** R S T U V W X Y Z

rabbit (RAB-it)

Spanish: conejo **Pilipino:** kuneho

Vietnamese: con thỏ **Chinese:** 兔子

Hmong: tus luav **French:** lapin

raccoon (ra-KOON)

Spanish: mapache **Pilipino:** rakoon

Vietnamese: con gấu trúc **Chinese:** 浣熊

Hmong: ntshuab **French:** raton laveur

racing car
(RAYS-ing kar)

Spanish: coche de carreras **Pilipino:** kotseng pangkarera

Vietnamese: xe đua **Chinese:** 赛车 / 賽車

Hmong: tsheb sib xeem **French:** voiture de course

radio (RAY-dee-oh)

Spanish: radio **Pilipino:** radio

Vietnamese: máy thu thanh **Chinese:** 收音机 / 收音機

Hmong: xov tooj cua **French:** radio

raincoat (RAYN-koht)

Spanish: impermeable **Pilipino:** kapote

Vietnamese: áo mưa **Chinese:** 雨衣

Hmong: tsho tiv nag **French:** imperméable

a b c d e f g h i j k l m n o p q r s t u v w x y z

Sounds Like Fun!

Rake rhymes with *cake*. Now it's your turn to make a rhyme. Think of a word that rhymes with *rat*. Ask a partner to guess the word.

---

rake (rayk)

Spanish: rastrillo   **Pilipino:** kalaykay

Vietnamese: cái cào   **Chinese:** 耙子

Hmong: pas hus nroj tsuag   **French:** râteau

---

rat (rat)

Spanish: rata   **Pilipino:** daga

Vietnamese: con chuột   **Chinese:** 鼠

Hmong: nas tsuag   **French:** rat

---

rectangle (REK-tayng-ul)

Spanish: rectángulo   **Pilipino:** parihaba

Vietnamese: hình chữ nhật   **Chinese:** 长方形 / 長方形

Hmong: rectangle   **French:** rectangle

---

red (red)

Spanish: rojo   **Pilipino:** pula

Vietnamese: màu đỏ   **Chinese:** 红 / 紅

Hmong: liab   **French:** rouge

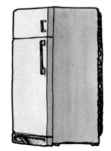

refrigerator
(rih-FRIJ-uh-ray-tur)

Spanish: refrigerador   **Pilipino:** pridyeder

Vietnamese: cái tủ lạnh   **Chinese:** 冰箱

Hmong: tub yees   **French:** réfrigérateur

A B C D E F G H I J K L M N O P Q R S T U V W X Y Z

rhinoceros
(ry-NAHS-ur-us)

Spanish: rinoceronte   **Pilipino:** rinoseros

Vietnamese: con tê giác   **Chinese:** 犀牛

Hmong: twj kum   **French:** rhinocéros

rice (rys)

Spanish: arroz   **Pilipino:** kanin

Vietnamese: cơm   **Chinese:** 米

Hmong: mov   **French:** riz

ring (ring)

Spanish: anillo   **Pilipino:** singsing

Vietnamese: cái nhẫn   **Chinese:** 戒指

Hmong: nplhaib   **French:** bague

river (RIV-ur)

Spanish: río   **Pilipino:** ilog

Vietnamese: con sông   **Chinese:** 河川

Hmong: tus dej   **French:** fleuve, rivière

road (rohd)

Spanish: carretera   **Pilipino:** daan

Vietnamese: con đường   **Chinese:** 道路

Hmong: txoj kev   **French:** route

a b c d e f g h i j k l m n o p q r s t u v w x y z

A
B
C
D
E
F
G
H
I
J
K
L
M
N
O
P
Q
R
S
T
U
V
W
X
Y
Z

robe (rohb)

Spanish: bata

Vietnamese: áo choàng

Hmong: lub tsho hnav npog

Pilipino: balabal

Chinese: 长外袍 / 長外袍

French: peignoir

rocket (RAHK-it)

Spanish: cohete

Vietnamese: hỏa tiển

Hmong: cua luaj

Pilipino: raket

Chinese: 火箭

French: fusée

roller skate
(ROHL-ur skayt)

Spanish: patín de ruedas

Vietnamese: giày có bánh xe để trượt

Hmong: khau log

Pilipino: gulong na isket, roler isket

Chinese: 旱冰鞋 / 溜冰鞋

French: patin à roulettes

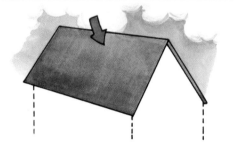

roof (roof)

Spanish: techo, tejado

Vietnamese: mái nhà

Hmong: ru tsev

Pilipino: bubong

Chinese: 屋顶 / 屋頂

French: toit

room (room)

Spanish: sala, salón

Vietnamese: căn phòng

Hmong: chav, hoob

Pilipino: kuwarto

Chinese: 房间 / 房間

French: salle

rooster (ROOS-tur)

Spanish: gallo　　　　**Pilipino:** tandang

Vietnamese: con gà trống　　**Chinese:** 雄鸡 / 雄雞

Hmong: lau qaib　　**French:** coq

ruler (ROO-lur)

Spanish: regla　　　　**Pilipino:** reglador

Vietnamese: cái thước　　**Chinese:** 尺

Hmong: pas ntsuas　　**French:** règle

a
b
c
d
e
f
g
h
i
j
k
l
m
n
o
p
q
r
s
t
u
v
w
x
y
z

Ss Ss

A B C D E F G H I J K L M N O P Q R **S** T U V W X Y Z

sailboat (SAYL-boht)

Spanish: barco de vela

Pilipino: batel

Vietnamese: thuyền buồm

Chinese: 帆船

Hmong: nko cua

French: bateau à voiles

salad (SAL-ud)

Spanish: ensalada

Pilipino: salad

Vietnamese: rau xà lách

Chinese: 生菜沙拉

Hmong: xa lav

French: salade

sales clerk (SAYLZ klurk)

Spanish: vendedor

Pilipino: tindera

Vietnamese: ngươi bán hàng

Chinese: 店员 / 店員

Hmong: tus muag khoom

French: vendeur

salt (sahlt)

Spanish: sal

Pilipino: asin

Vietnamese: muối

Chinese: 盐 / 鹽

Hmong: ntsev

French: sel

sandbox (SAND-bahks)

Spanish: cajón de arena

Pilipino: larnan ng buhangin

Vietnamese: hộp cát

Chinese: 沙盒

Hmong: thawv xuab zeeb

French: bac à sable

Dictionary Detective

Saturday is one of the days of the week. Look at the table of contents. Which page tells you <u>all</u> the days of the week?

sandwich (SAND-wich)

Spanish: emparedado

Vietnamese: bánh mì săn quých

Hmong: sandwich

Pilipino: sanwits

Chinese: 三明治

French: sandwich

Saturday (SAT-ur-day)

Spanish: sábado

Vietnamese: Thứ Bảy

Hmong: Saturday

Pilipino: Sabado

Chinese: 星期六

French: samedi

saw (sah)

Spanish: sierra, serrucho

Vietnamese: cái cưa

Hmong: kaw

Pilipino: lagari

Chinese: 锯子 / 鋸子

French: scie

school bus (SKOOL bus)

Spanish: autobús escolar

Vietnamese: xe buýt học đường

Hmong: npav thauj me nyuam kawm ntawv

Pilipino: bus na pangeskuwela

Chinese: 校车 / 校車

French: autobus scolaire

---

scissors (SIZ-urz)

Spanish: tijeras

Vietnamese: cái kéo

Hmong: rab txiab

Pilipino: gunting

Chinese: 剪刀

French: ciseaux

a b c d e f g h i j k l m n o p q r **s** t u v w x y z

sea (see)

Spanish: mar
Pilipino: dagat

Vietnamese: biển
Chinese: 海

Hmong: dej hiav txwv
French: mer

sea horse (SEE hors)

Spanish: caballo de mar
Pilipino: kabayong-dagat

Vietnamese: con hải mã
Chinese: 海马 / 海馬

Hmong: nees dej
French: hippocampe

seal (seel)

Spanish: foca
Pilipino: poka

Vietnamese: con hải cẩu
Chinese: 海狗

Hmong: ntshuab deg
French: phoque

sea turtle (see TUR-tul)

Spanish: tortuga del mar
Pilipino: pawikan

Vietnamese: con rùa biển
Chinese: 海龟 / 海龜

Hmong: vaub kib dej
French: tortue de mer

second (SEK-und)

Spanish: segundo
Pilipino: pangalawa

Vietnamese: thứ nhì
Chinese: 第二

Hmong: thib ob
French: second

secretary
(SEK-ruh-tayr-ee)

Spanish: secretaria   **Pilipino:** sekretarya

Vietnamese: thư ký   **Chinese:** 秘书／秘書

Hmong: tus khaws ntaub ntawv   **French:** secrétaire

September
(sep-TEM-bur)

Spanish: septiembre   **Pilipino:** Setyembre

Vietnamese: Tháng Chín   **Chinese:** 九月

Hmong: cuaj hli ntuj   **French:** septembre

7

seven tops

seven (SEV-un)

Spanish: siete   **Pilipino:** pito

Vietnamese: bảy   **Chinese:** 七

Hmong: xya   **French:** sept

17

seventeen butterflies

seventeen
(sev-un-TEEN)

Spanish: diecisiete   **Pilipino:** labimpito

Vietnamese: mười bảy   **Chinese:** 十七

Hmong: kaum xya   **French:** dix-sept

seventh (SEV-unth)

Spanish: séptimo   **Pilipino:** ikapito

Vietnamese: thứ bảy   **Chinese:** 第七

Hmong: thib xya   **French:** septième

a b c d e f g h i j k l m n o p q r **s** t u v w x y z

103

A B C D E F G H I J K L M N O P Q R **S** T U V W X Y Z

seventy (SEV-un-tee)

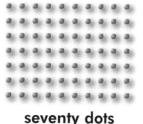

70

seventy dots

Spanish: setenta

Vietnamese: bảy mươi

Hmong: xya caum

Pilipino: pitumpu

Chinese: 七十

French: soixante-dix

sewing machine (SOH-ing muh-SHEEN)

Spanish: máquina de costura

Vietnamese: máy may

Hmong: tshuab xaws khaub ncaws

Pilipino: makinang pangtahe

Chinese: 裁缝机 / 裁縫機

French: machine à coudre

shark (shark)

Spanish: tiburón

Vietnamese: con cá mập

Hmong: shark

Pilipino: pating

Chinese: 鲨鱼 / 鯊魚

French: requin

sheep (sheep)

Spanish: oveja

Vietnamese: con cừu

Hmong: yaj

Pilipino: tupa

Chinese: 羊

French: mouton

shell (shel)

Spanish: concha

Vietnamese: con sò

Hmong: pliag deg

Pilipino: kabibi

Chinese: 贝壳 / 貝殼

French: coquillage

Dictionary Detective

All the words on this page begin with the letters s and h. Find two words in this book that begin with "b" and end with "sh." What are they?

ship (ship)

Spanish: barco, buque   **Pilipino:** barko

Vietnamese: chiếc tàu   **Chinese:** 船

Hmong: lub nkoj loj   **French:** bateau

shirt (shurt)

Spanish: camisa   **Pilipino:** kamisadentro

Vietnamese: áo sơ mi   **Chinese:** 衬衫 / 襯衫

Hmong: lub tsho   **French:** chemisier, chemise

shoe (shoo)

Spanish: zapato   **Pilipino:** sapatos

Vietnamese: giày   **Chinese:** 鞋

Hmong: khau   **French:** chaussure

shorts (shorts)

Spanish: pantalones cortos   **Pilipino:** maikling pantalon

Vietnamese: quần ngắn   **Chinese:** 短裤 / 短褲

Hmong: ris luv   **French:** shorts

shoulder (SHOHL-dur)

Spanish: hombro   **Pilipino:** balikat

Vietnamese: cái vai   **Chinese:** 肩膀

Hmong: xwb pwg   **French:** épaule

a b c d e f g h i j k l m n o p q r **s** t u v w x y z

A B C D E F G H I J K L M N O P Q R **S** T U V W X Y Z

shovel (SHUV-ul)

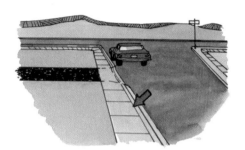

Spanish: pala

Pilipino: pala

Vietnamese: cái xẻng

Chinese: 铲子 / 鏟子

Hmong: hlau yawm av, rab luab

French: pelle

sidewalk (SYD-wahk)

Spanish: acera

Pilipino: bangketa

Vietnamese: lối đi bộ

Chinese: 人行道

Hmong: ntug kev

French: trottoir

sink (sink)

Spanish: fregadero

Pilipino: lababo

Vietnamese: cái bồn

Chinese: 洗手池

Hmong: dab ntxuav tes

French: évier

sister (SIS-tur)

Spanish: hermana

Pilipino: kapatid na babae

Vietnamese: chị, em gái

Chinese: 姊妹

Hmong: niam laus, niam hluas, viv ncaus, muam

French: sœur

six (siks)

6

six strawberries

Spanish: seis

Pilipino: anim

Vietnamese: sáu

Chinese: 六

Hmong: rau

French: six

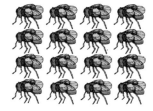

sixteen (siks-TEEN)

16

sixteen flies

Spanish: dieciséis	**Pilipino:** labing-anim
Vietnamese: mười sáu	**Chinese:** 十六
Hmong: kaum rau	**French:** seize

sixth (siksth)

Spanish: sexto	**Pilipino:** ikaanim
Vietnamese: thứ sáu	**Chinese:** 第六
Hmong: thib rau	**French:** sixième

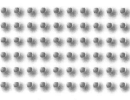

sixty (SIKS-tee)

60

sixty dots

Spanish: sesenta	**Pilipino:** animnapu
Vietnamese: sáu mươi	**Chinese:** 六十
Hmong: rau caum	**French:** soixante

skateboard (SKAYT-bord)

Spanish: patineta, monopatín	**Pilipino:** isketbord
Vietnamese: ván trượt	**Chinese:** 溜冰板
Hmong: skateboard	**French:** planche à roulettes

skin (skin)

Spanish: piel	**Pilipino:** balat
Vietnamese: da	**Chinese:** 皮肤／皮膚
Hmong: tawv nqaij	**French:** peau

a b c d e f g h i j k l m n o p q r **s** t u v w x y z

skirt (skurt)

Spanish: falda

Pilipino: saya

Vietnamese: cái váy

Chinese: 裙子

Hmong: daim tiab

French: jupe

skunk (skunk)

Spanish: zorrillo, mofeta

Pilipino: mabahong hayop kapag nagulat

Vietnamese: con chồn hôi

Chinese: 臭鼬鼠

Hmong: skunk

French: moufette

sky (sky)

Spanish: cielo

Pilipino: langit

Vietnamese: bầu trời

Chinese: 天空

Hmong: saum ntuj

French: ciel

slide (slyd)

Spanish: resbaladero

Pilipino: magpadulas

Vietnamese: ván trượt

Chinese: 滑板 / 溜滑梯

Hmong: zawv zawg

French: toboggan

slipper (SLIP-ur)

Spanish: pantufla, zapatilla

Pilipino: tsinelas

Vietnamese: dép lê

Chinese: 拖鞋

Hmong: khau rau hauv tsev

French: pantouffle

A
B
C
D
E
F
G
H
I
J
K
L
M
N
O
P
Q
R
S
T
U
V
W
X
Y
Z

Sounds Like Fun!

Go on a two-minute word hunt with a friend.
Start the clock and in two minutes find as many
things as you can that start with the letter s.

snail (snayl)

Spanish: caracol   **Pilipino:** kuhol

Vietnamese: con ốc sên   **Chinese:** 蜗牛／蝸牛

Hmong: qwj yeeg   **French:** escargot

snake (snayk)

Spanish: serpiente   **Pilipino:** ahas

Vietnamese: con rắn   **Chinese:** 蛇

Hmong: nab   **French:** serpent

soap (sohp)

Spanish: jabón   **Pilipino:** sabon

Vietnamese: xà phòng   **Chinese:** 肥皂

Hmong: xu npus   **French:** savon

soccer ball
(SAHK-ur bahl)

Spanish: bola de fútbol   **Pilipino:** saker

Vietnamese: banh túc cầu   **Chinese:** 足球

Hmong: npas ncaws, pob ncaws   **French:** ballon de football

sock (sahk)

Spanish: calcetín   **Pilipino:** medyas

Vietnamese: bi thất ngắn   **Chinese:** 袜子／襪子

Hmong: tham khwm   **French:** chaussette

a b c d e f g h i j k l m n o p q r **s** t u v w x y z

A B C D E F G H I J K L M N O P Q R **S** T U V W X Y Z

soda (SOH-duh)

Spanish: soda   **Pilipino:** soda

Vietnamese: sô đa   **Chinese:** 汽水

Hmong: dej qab zib   **French:** boisson gazeuse

sofa (SOH-fuh)

Spanish: sofá   **Pilipino:** supa

Vietnamese: ghế nệm dài   **Chinese:** 沙发椅 / 沙發椅

Hmong: roojzaum   **French:** canapé

soldier (SOHL-jur)

Spanish: soldado   **Pilipino:** sundalo

Vietnamese: người lính   **Chinese:** 军人 / 軍人

Hmong: tub nrog   **French:** soldat

soup (soop)

Spanish: sopa   **Pilipino:** sabaw

Vietnamese: canh   **Chinese:** 汤 / 湯

Hmong: kua zaub, kua nqaij   **French:** potage

space capsule
(spays KAP-sul)

Spanish: cápsula espacial   **Pilipino:** kapsulang pangkalawakan

Vietnamese: khoang tàu vũ trụ   **Chinese:** 太空舱 / 太空艙

Hmong: space capsule   **French:** capsule spatiale

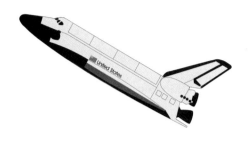

space shuttle
(spays SHUT-ul)

Spanish: transbordador especial

Pilipino: sasakyang pangkalawakan

Vietnamese: tàu con thoi

Chinese: 太空船

Hmong: lub nyooj hoom mus saum ntuj

French: navette spatiale

spaghetti (spuh-GET-ee)

Spanish: espagueti

Pilipino: spagheti

Vietnamese: mì ống

Chinese: 细通心面 / 細通心麵

Hmong: spaghetti

French: spaghetti

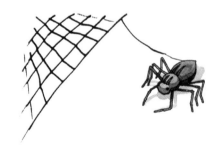

spider (SPY-dur)

Spanish: araña

Pilipino: gagamba

Vietnamese: con nhện

Chinese: 蜘蛛

Hmong: kab laug sab

French: araignée

spinach (SPIN-ich)

Spanish: espinaca

Pilipino: espinaka

Vietnamese: rau bó xôi

Chinese: 菠菜

Hmong: ib hom zaub

French: épinards

spoon (spoon)

Spanish: cuchara

Pilipino: kutsara

Vietnamese: cái muỗng

Chinese: 匙

Hmong: diav

French: cuillère

A
B
C
D
E
F
G
H
I
J
K
L
M
N
O
P
Q
R
S
T
U
V
W
X
Y
Z

spring (spring)

Spanish: primavera   **Pilipino:** tag-sibol

Vietnamese: mùa xuân   **Chinese:** 春

Hmong: ncaij nplooj ntoos hlav   **French:** printemps

square (skwayr)

Spanish: cuadrado   **Pilipino:** parisukat

Vietnamese: hình vuông   **Chinese:** 正方

Hmong: plaub ces kaum ntev sib luag   **French:** carré

squirrel (skwurl)

Spanish: ardilla   **Pilipino:** ardilya

Vietnamese: con sóc   **Chinese:** 松鼠

Hmong: nas ncuav   **French:** écureuil

stairs (stayrz)

Spanish: escaleras   **Pilipino:** hagdan

Vietnamese: thang lầu   **Chinese:** 楼梯 / 樓梯

Hmong: ntaiv   **French:** escalier

star (star)

Spanish: estrella   **Pilipino:** bituin

Vietnamese: ngôi sao   **Chinese:** 星

Hmong: hnub qub   **French:** étoile

Sounds Like Fun!

What do you get when you take the *star* out of *starfish*? What do you get when you take the *berry* out of *strawberry*? Now ask a friend these questions.

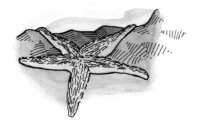

starfish (STAR-fish)

Spanish: estrellamar   **Pilipino:** isdang-bituin

Vietnamese: con sao biển   **Chinese:** 海星

Hmong: ntses hnub qub   **French:** étoile de mer

station wagon (STAY-shun WAG-un)

Spanish: furgoneta familiar   **Pilipino:** station wagon

Vietnamese: xe có chỗ để hành lý phí sau   **Chinese:** 小厢型车／小廂型車

Hmong: tsheb   **French:** break

stomach (STUM-uk)

Spanish: estómago   **Pilipino:** tiyan

Vietnamese: bao tử   **Chinese:** 肚子

Hmong: lub plab   **French:** estomac

stove (stohv)

Spanish: estufa   **Pilipino:** kalan

Vietnamese: bếp lò   **Chinese:** 炉子／爐子

Hmong: qhov cub   **French:** fourneau, cuisinière

strawberry (STRAH-bayr-ee)

Spanish: fresa   **Pilipino:** istroberi

Vietnamese: trái dâu   **Chinese:** 草莓

Hmong: strawberry   **French:** fraise

a b c d e f g h i j k l m n o p q r **s** t u v w x y z

street (street)

Spanish: calle

Pilipino: daan

Vietnamese: đường phố

Chinese: 街道

Hmong: kev

French: rue

submarine (SUB-muh-reen)

Spanish: submarino

Pilipino: submarino

Vietnamese: tàu ngầm

Chinese: 潜水艇 / 潛水艇

Hmong: nkoj mus hauv qab thu dej

French: sous-marin

suit (soot)

Spanish: traje

Pilipino: terno

Vietnamese: bột đồ vét

Chinese: 西装 / 西裝

Hmong: suit

French: costume

summer (SUM-ur)

Spanish: verano

Pilipino: tag-araw

Vietnamese: mùa hè

Chinese: 夏

Hmong: caij ntuj sov

French: été

Sunday (SUN-day)

Spanish: domingo

Pilipino: Linggo

Vietnamese: Chủ Nhật

Chinese: 星期日

Hmong: Sunday

French: dimanche

sweater (SWET-ur)

Spanish: suéter

Pilipino: suweter

Vietnamese: áo len cổ chui

Chinese: 毛衣

Hmong: tsho tuaj plaub sov

French: pull-over

sweet potato
(sweet puh-TAY-toh)

Spanish: batata

Pilipino: kamote

Vietnamese: khoai lang

Chinese: 红薯 / 地瓜

Hmong: qos liab

French: patate douce

swing (swing)

Spanish: columpio

Pilipino: duyan

Vietnamese: cái đu

Chinese: 秋千 / 鞦韆

Hmong: viav vias

French: balançoire

a b c d e f g h i j k l m n o p q r **s** t u v w x y z

table (TAY-bul)

Spanish: mesa

Pilipino: mesa

Vietnamese: cái bàn

Chinese: 桌子

Hmong: rooj

French: table

taco (TAH-coh)

Spanish: taco

Pilipino: tako

Vietnamese: bánh tráng kẹp thịt

Chinese: 墨西哥食物

Hmong: taco

French: taco

tape player (tayp PLAY-ur)

Spanish: tocacintas, grabadora

Pilipino: tugtugan ng teyp

Vietnamese: máy hát băng

Chinese: 录音机 / 錄放音機

Hmong: lub thev

French: lecteur de cassettes

teacher (TEE-chur)

Spanish: profesor, maestro

Pilipino: guro

Vietnamese: thầy giáo

Chinese: 教师 / 教師

Hmong: kws qhia ntawv, xib fwb, nai ku

French: professeur

teapot (TEE-paht)

Spanish: tetera

Pilipino: tsarera

Vietnamese: bình trà

Chinese: 茶壶 / 茶壺

Hmong: hwj kais

French: théière

telephone
(TEL-uh-fohn)

Spanish: teléfono   **Pilipino:** telepono

Vietnamese: điện thoại   **Chinese:** 电话 / 電話

Hmong: xov tooj   **French:** téléphone

television
(TEL-uh-vih-zhun)

Spanish: televisión, televisor   **Pilipino:** telebisyon

Vietnamese: máy truyền hình   **Chinese:** 电视[机] / 電視機

Hmong: t.v.   **French:** télévision

10

ten balls

ten (ten)

Spanish: diez   **Pilipino:** sampu

Vietnamese: mười   **Chinese:** 十

Hmong: kaum   **French:** dix

tenth (tenth)

Spanish: décimo   **Pilipino:** pansampu

Vietnamese: thứ mười   **Chinese:** 第十

Hmong: thib kaum   **French:** dixième

third (thurd)

Spanish: tercero   **Pilipino:** pangatlo

Vietnamese: thứ ba   **Chinese:** 第三

Hmong: ntib peb   **French:** troisième

a b c d e f g h i j k l m n o p q r s t u v w x y z

Dictionary Detective

Find three food words that begin with the letter p. What are they?

---

thirteen (thur-TEEN)

13

thirteen erasers

Spanish: trece	**Pilipino:** labing-tatlo
Vietnamese: mười ba	**Chinese:** 十三
Hmong: kaum peb	**French:** treize

---

thirty (THUR-tee)

30

thirty dots

Spanish: treinta	**Pilipino:** tatlumpu
Vietnamese: ba mươi	**Chinese:** 三十
Hmong: peb caug	**French:** trente

---

three (three)

3

three chicks

Spanish: tres	**Pilipino:** tatlo
Vietnamese: ba	**Chinese:** 三
Hmong: peb	**French:** trois

---

thumb (thum)

Spanish: pulgar	**Pilipino:** hinlalaki
Vietnamese: ngón tay cái	**Chinese:** 拇指
Hmong: ntiv tes xoo	**French:** pouce

Thursday (THURZ-day)

Spanish: jueves	**Pilipino:** Huwebes
Vietnamese: Thứ Năm	**Chinese:** 星期四
Hmong: Thursday	**French:** jeudi

tiger (TY-gur)

Spanish: tigre

Pilipino: tigre

Vietnamese: con cọp

Chinese: 虎

Hmong: tsov

French: tigre

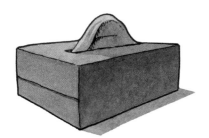

tissue (TISH-oo)

Spanish: pañuelo de papel

Pilipino: tisyu

Vietnamese: giấy lau mềm

Chinese: 纸巾 / 紙巾

Hmong: ntaub so ntswg

French: mouchoir en papier

toast (tohst)

Spanish: pan tostado

Pilipino: brindis

Vietnamese: bánh mì nướng

Chinese: 吐司面包 / 吐司麵包

Hmong: toast

French: toast

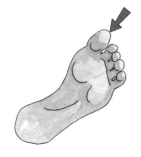

toe (toh)

Spanish: dedo del pie

Pilipino: daliri sa paa

Vietnamese: ngón chân

Chinese: 脚趾 / 腳指

Hmong: ntiv taw xoo,
ntiv taw thawj

French: orteil

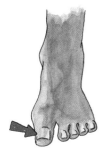

toenail (TOH-nayl)

Spanish: uña del dedo del pie

Pilipino: kuko sa paa

Vietnamese: móng chân

Chinese: 脚趾甲 / 腳指甲

Hmong: rau taw

French: ongle d'orteil

a b c d e f g h i j k l m n o p q r s t u v w x y z

119

A
B
C
D
E
F
G
H
I
J
K
L
M
N
O
P
Q
R
S
T
U
V
W
X
Y
Z

toilet (TOY-lit)

Spanish: inodoro, lavabo **Pilipino:** banyo

Vietnamese: nhà vệ sinh **Chinese:** 马桶 / 馬桶

Hmong: chaw zaum tawm rooj, **French:** toilette
qhov viv

tomato (tuh-MAY-toh)

Spanish: tomate **Pilipino:** kamatis

Vietnamese: cà chua **Chinese:** 蕃茄

Hmong: txiv lws liab, **French:** tomate
txiv lws suav

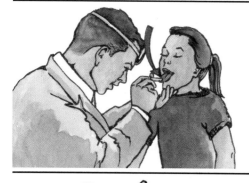

tongue (tung)

Spanish: lengua **Pilipino:** dila

Vietnamese: cái lưỡi **Chinese:** 舌

Hmong: plaig **French:** langue

tools

tool (tool)

Spanish: herramienta **Pilipino:** kasangkapan

Vietnamese: dụng cụ **Chinese:** 工具

Hmong: ciaj **French:** outil

tooth (tooth)

Spanish: diente **Pilipino:** ngipin

Vietnamese: cái răng **Chinese:** 牙齿 / 牙齒

Hmong: kaus hniav **French:** dent

toothbrush
(TOOTH-brush)

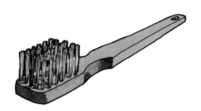

Spanish: cepillo de dientes

Pilipino: sepilyo sa ngipin

Vietnamese: bàn chải răng

Chinese: 牙刷

Hmong: tus txhuam hniav

French: brosse à dents

toothpaste
(TOOTH-payst)

Spanish: pasta dental

Pilipino: kremang pansipilyo

Vietnamese: kem đánh răng

Chinese: 牙膏

Hmong: tshuaj txhuam hniav

French: dentifrice

top (tahp)

Spanish: trompo

Pilipino: turompo

Vietnamese: con vụ

Chinese: 陀螺

Hmong: tu lub

French: toupie

tow truck (toh truk)

Spanish: carro de remolque, grúa

Pilipino: trak pang hatak

Vietnamese: xe dùng để kéo xe khác

Chinese: 拖车／拖吊車

Hmong: tsheb cab

French: dépanneuse

towel (TOU-ul)

Spanish: toalla

Pilipino: tuwalya

Vietnamese: khăn tắm, khăn lau

Chinese: 毛巾

Hmong: phuam

French: serviette

a b c d e f g h i j k l m n o p q r s t u v w x y z

121

A
B
C
D
E
F
G
H
I
J
K
L
M
N
O
P
Q
R
S
T
U
V
W
X
Y
Z

trailer (TRAY-lur)

Spanish: remolque

Pilipino: treyler

Vietnamese: toa móc

Chinese: 拖车／拖曳車

Hmong: lub laub cab tom qab

French: remorque

train (trayn)

Spanish: tren

Pilipino: tren

Vietnamese: xe lửa

Chinese: 火车／火車

Hmong: tsheb ciav hlau

French: train

trash can (trash kan)

Spanish: cesto de la basura

Pilipino: basura

Vietnamese: thùng đựng rác

Chinese: 垃圾筒

Hmong: thoob khib nyiab

French: poubelle

trash collector
(trash kuh-LEK-tur)

Spanish: colector de la basura

Pilipino: basurero

Vietnamese: xe lấy rác

Chinese: 清洁工／清潔隊員

Hmong: tus neeg thauj khib nyiab

French: éboueur

tree (tree)

Spanish: árbol

Pilipino: puno

Vietnamese: cây

Chinese: 树木／樹木

Hmong: ntoo

French: arbre

triangle (TRY-ayng-gul)

Spanish: triángulo

Pilipino: tatsulok

Vietnamese: hình tam giác

Chinese: 三角形

Hmong: peb ceg

French: triangle

tricycle (TRY-sik-ul)

Spanish: triciclo

Pilipino: trisiklo, traysikel

Vietnamese: xe đạp ba bánh

Chinese: 三轮脚踏车 / 三輪車

Hmong: luv thim peb lub log

French: tricycle

truck (truk)

Spanish: camioneta, camión

Pilipino: trak

Vietnamese: xe tải

Chinese: 卡车 / 卡車

Hmong: truck

French: camionnette, camion

truck driver (truk DRY-vur)

Spanish: camionero

Pilipino: tsuper ng trak

Vietnamese: tài xế xe tải

Chinese: 卡车驾驶员 / 卡車駕駛員

Hmong: tus neeg tshav (truck)

French: conducteur de camion

Tuesday (TOOZ-day)

Spanish: martes

Pilipino: Martes

Vietnamese: Thứ Ba

Chinese: 星期二

Hmong: Tuesday

French: mardi

a b c d e f g h i j k l m n o p q r s t u v w x y z

A
B
C
D
E
F
G
H
I
J
K
L
M
N
O
P
Q
R
S
T
U
V
W
X
Y
Z

Dictionary Detective

Two words in this book begin with the letter x.
What are they?

turkey (TUR-kee)

Spanish: pavo **Pilipino:** pabo

Vietnamese: gà tây **Chinese:** 火鸡／火雞

Hmong: qaib ntxhw **French:** dinde

turtle (TUR-tul)

Spanish: tortuga **Pilipino:** pagong

Vietnamese: con rùa **Chinese:** 乌龟／烏龜

Hmong: vaub kib **French:** tortue

12
twelve pencils

twelve (twelv)

Spanish: doce **Pilipino:** labindalawa

Vietnamese: mười hai **Chinese:** 十二

Hmong: kaum ob **French:** douze

20
twenty dots

twenty (TWEN-tee)

Spanish: veinte **Pilipino:** dalawampu

Vietnamese: hai mươi **Chinese:** 二十

Hmong: nees nkaum **French:** vingt

2

two cupcakes

two (too)

Spanish: dos **Pilipino:** dalawa

Vietnamese: hai **Chinese:** 二

Hmong: ob **French:** deux

typewriter (TYP-ryt-ur)

Spanish: máquina de escribir

Pilipino: makinilya

Vietnamese: máy đánh chữ

Chinese: 打字机／打字機

Hmong: tshuab ntaus ntawv

French: machine à écrire

Uu Uu

umbrella (um-BREL-uh)

Spanish: paraguas

Pilipino: payong

Vietnamese: cây dù

Chinese: 伞 / 傘

Hmong: lub kaus

French: parapluie

uncle (UN-kul)

Spanish: tío

Pilipino: tiyo

Vietnamese: cậu, chú, bác

Chinese: 伯父,叔父,姑父,姨丈 / 伯父,叔父,姑丈,姨丈

Hmong: dab laug, txiv hlob, txiv ntxawm

French: oncle

underwear (UN-dur-wayr)

Spanish: ropa interior

Pilipino: pangilalim

Vietnamese: đồ lót

Chinese: 内衣裤 / 內衣褲

Hmong: ris tshos xuab

French: sous-vêtements

vacuum cleaner
(VAK-yoom KLEEN-ur)

Spanish: aspiradora

Pilipino: bakyum

Vietnamese: máy hút bụi

Chinese: 吸尘器 / 吸塵器

Hmong: cav qus tsev

French: aspirateur

van (van)

Spanish: furgoneta, camioneta

Pilipino: ban

Vietnamese: xe van

Chinese: 行理车 / 行李車

Hmong: lub vees

French: camionnette

VCR (vee-see-AR)

Spanish: VCR

Pilipino: VCR

Vietnamese: máy chiếu video

Chinese: 录像机 / 錄影機

Hmong: lub VCR

French: magnétoscope

veterinarian
(vet-ur-uh-NAYR-ee-un)

Spanish: veterinario

Pilipino: beterinaryo

Vietnamese: bác sĩ thú y

Chinese: 兽医 / 獸醫

Hmong: kws kho tsiaj mob

French: vétérinaire

videotape
(VID-ee-oh-tayp)

Spanish: videocinta, cinta magnética para grabar

Pilipino: vidiyo

Vietnamese: băng video

Chinese: 录像带 / 錄影帶

Hmong: ka xev

French: vidéocassette

a
b
c
d
e
f
g
h
i
j
k
l
m
n
o
p
q
r
s
t
u
v
w
x
y
z

Ww Ww

wagon (WA-gun)

Spanish: vagoneta

Pilipino: karo

Vietnamese: toa xe

Chinese: 小拖车 / 小拖車

Hmong: lub laub

French: charrette

waist (wayst)

Spanish: cintura

Pilipino: baywang

Vietnamese: eo, chỗ thắt lưng

Chinese: 腰部

Hmong: duav

French: taille

waiter (WAY-tur)

Spanish: camarero, mesero

Pilipino: serbidor

Vietnamese: người hầu bàn

Chinese: 侍者

Hmong: tus txiv neej nqa zaub tom lab no mov

French: serveur

waitress (WAY-tris)

Spanish: camarera, mesera

Pilipino: serbidora

Vietnamese: nữ hầu bàn

Chinese: 女侍

Hmong: tus poj niam nqa zaub tom lab noj mov

French: serveuse

washcloth (WAHSH-kloth)

Spanish: toallita para lavarse

Pilipino: bimpo

Vietnamese: khăn lau mặt

Chinese: 毛巾

Hmong: phuam ntxuav muag

French: gant de toilette

a
b
c
d
e
f
g
h
i
j
k
l
m
n
o
p
q
r
s
t
u
v
w
x
y
z

washing machine
(WAHSH-ing muh-SHEEN)

Spanish: lavadora

Pilipino: makinang pang laba

Vietnamese: máy giặt

Chinese: 洗衣机 / 洗衣機

Hmong: tshuab ntxhua khaub ncaws

French: machine à laver

wastebasket
(WAYST-bas-kit)

Spanish: cesto de los papeles

Pilipino: basurahang basket

Vietnamese: sọt rác

Chinese: 废纸篓 / 廢紙簍

Hmong: thoob khib nyiab

French: corbeille à papier

watch (wahch)

Spanish: reloj

Pilipino: relos

Vietnamese: cái đồng hồ

Chinese: 手表 / 手錶

Hmong: moos

French: montre

water (WAH-tur)

Spanish: agua

Pilipino: tubig

Vietnamese: nước

Chinese: 水

Hmong: dej

French: eau

watermelon
(WAH-tur-mel-un)

Spanish: sandía

Pilipino: pakwan

Vietnamese: trái dưa hấu

Chinese: 西瓜

Hmong: dib liab

French: pastèque

web site (web syt)

Spanish: sitio web, página de Internet

Vietnamese: trang mạng

Hmong: web site

Pilipino: web site

Chinese: 网站 / 網站

French: site web

Wednesday (WENZ-day)

Spanish: miércoles

Vietnamese: Thứ Tư

Hmong: Wednesday

Pilipino: Miyerkules

Chinese: 星期三

French: mercredi

whale (wayl)

Spanish: ballena

Vietnamese: con cá voi

Hmong: ib hom ntses loj

Pilipino: balyena

Chinese: 鲸鱼 / 鯨魚

French: baleine

wheel (weel)

Spanish: rueda, llanta

Vietnamese: bánh xe

Hmong: thob log

Pilipino: gulong

Chinese: 轮 / 輪

French: roue

whistle (WIS-ul)

Spanish: silbato, pito

Vietnamese: cái còi

Hmong: lub pib tshuab

Pilipino: silbato

Chinese: 口哨 / 口哨

French: siffler

Dictionary Detective

White is a color. Find the word in this book that is a color which ends in the letter w. What is it?

white (wyt)

Spanish: blanco

Pilipino: puti

Vietnamese: màu trắng

Chinese: 白色

Hmong: dawb

French: blanc

window (WIN-doh)

Spanish: ventana

Pilipino: bintana

Vietnamese: cửa sổ

Chinese: 窗

Hmong: qhov rai

French: fenêtre

winter (WIN-tur)

Spanish: invierno

Pilipino: taglamig

Vietnamese: mùa đông

Chinese: 冬

Hmong: caij ntuj no

French: hiver

wolf (woolf)

Spanish: lobo

Pilipino: lobo

Vietnamese: chó sói

Chinese: 狼

Hmong: ob qus

French: loup

woman (WUM-un)

Spanish: mujer

Pilipino: babae

Vietnamese: người đàn bà

Chinese: 女子

Hmong: poj niam

French: femme

a b c d e f g h i j k l m n o p q r s t u v **w** x y z

A
B
C
D
E
F
G
H
I
J
K
L
M
N
O
P
Q
R
S
T
U
V
W
X
Y
Z

worm (wurm)

Spanish: gusano

Pilipino: bulati

Vietnamese: con sâu

Chinese: 虫 / 蟲

Hmong: cua nab

French: ver

wrist (rist)

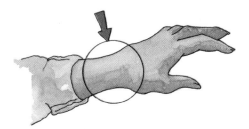

Spanish: muñeca

Pilipino: pupulsuhan

Vietnamese: cổ tay

Chinese: 手腕

Hmong: dab teg

French: poignet

x-ray (EKS-ray)

Spanish: radiografía

Vietnamese: tia x

Hmong: xoo fai fab

Pilipino: eks ray

Chinese: X射线 ╱ X光線

French: rayon X

xylophone
(ZY-luh-fohn)

Spanish: xilófono

Vietnamese: đàn gõ

Hmong: xylophone

Pilipino: saylopon

Chinese: 木琴

French: xylophone

a
b
c
d
e
f
g
h
i
j
k
l
m
n
o
p
q
r
s
t
u
v
w
x
y
z

Yy Yy Yy

yam (yam)

Spanish: ñame

Vietnamese: khoai từ, khoai mỡ

Hmong: qos liab

Pilipino: tugi

Chinese: 红薯 / 地瓜

French: patate douce

yard (yard)

Spanish: patio

Vietnamese: cái sân

Hmong: tog tsev

Pilipino: bakuran

Chinese: 庭院

French: cour

yarn (yarn)

Spanish: hilado

Vietnamese: sợi chỉ

Hmong: paws ntuag, xov paj

Pilipino: sinulid

Chinese: 纱 / 紗

French: laine

yellow (YEL-oh)

Spanish: amarillo

Vietnamese: màu vàng

Hmong: daj

Pilipino: dilaw

Chinese: 黄色

French: jaune

zebra (ZEE-bruh)

Spanish: cebra

Pilipino: sebra

Vietnamese: con ngựa vằn

Chinese: 斑马 / 斑馬

Hmong: nees txaij

French: zèbre

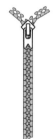

zipper (ZIP-ur)

Spanish: cremallera, cierre

Pilipino: siper

Vietnamese: khóa kéo

Chinese: 拉链 / 拉鍊

Hmong: txoj swb

French: fermeture éclair

zoo (zoo)

Spanish: parque zoológico

Pilipino: soolohiko

Vietnamese: sở thú

Chinese: 动物园 / 動物園

Hmong: chaw yug tsiaj hav zoov

French: zoo

zucchini (zoo-KEE-nee)

Spanish: calabacín

Pilipino: kalabasa

Vietnamese: bí xanh nhỏ

Chinese: 意大利南瓜 / 意大利瓜

Hmong: taub ntev

French: courgette

NUMBERS

Numbers 1-20

1
2
3
4
5

6
7
8
9
10

11
12
13
14
15

16
17
18
19
20

Numbers by Tens to 100

10   60

20   70

30   80

40   90

50   100

Ordinal Numbers

tenth

ninth
eighth
seventh

sixth

fifth
fourth

third

second

first

COLORS

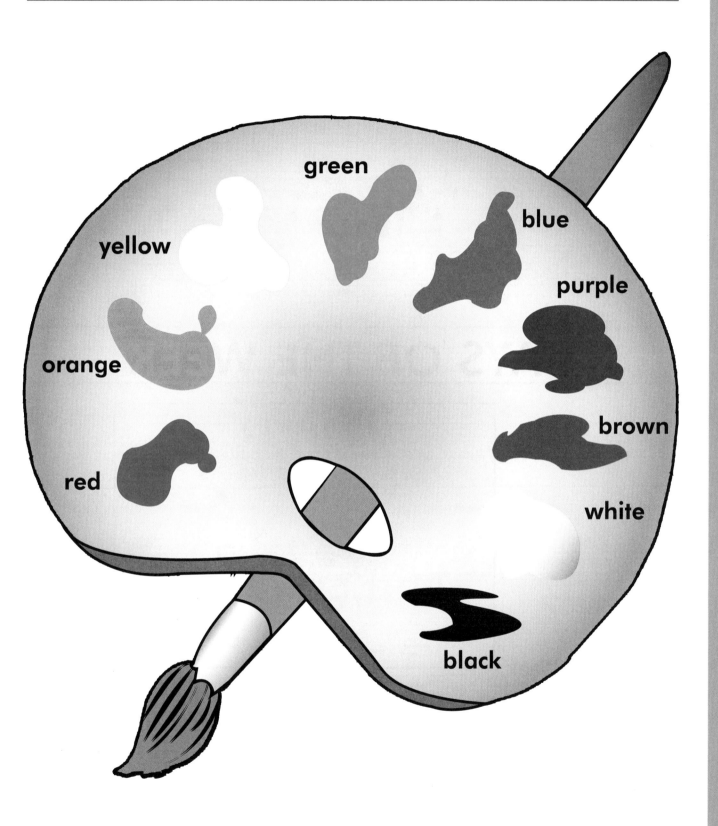

MONTHS OF THE YEAR

DAYS OF THE WEEK

January

Days of the Week →

Sunday	Monday	Tuesday	Wednesday	Thursday	Friday	Saturday
	1	2	3	4	5	6
7	8	9	10	11	12	13
14	15	16	17	18	19	20
21	22	23	24	25	26	27
28	29	30	31			

A Note to Teachers and Parents

Learning new words can be challenging for students, but give them a picture that illustrates the word and the task becomes much easier. Colorful illustrations capture the interest and imagination of students, making them more engaged in learning. The *IDEA Picture Dictionary* introduces students to basic vocabulary and gives them a foundation of dictionary and word attack skills. By developing these key skills, students will experience greater success as they learn to read.

The *IDEA Picture Dictionary* is easy to use. Entries are organized alphabetically, with letters down the side of each page and large letters marking the start of each section. Each entry includes a picture, English pronunciation*, and translations of the word into six languages. Throughout the dictionary you will find "✎Sounds Like Fun" activities to build students' understanding of sounds and "✐Dictionary Detective" activities to put their dictionary skills to work.

Using the *IDEA Picture Dictionary*

The *IDEA Picture Dictionary* can be used on its own or in conjunction with any English language development program, including *Carousel of IDEAS* and *IDEAS for Literature*.

To help students learn how to use the dictionary, read the introduction on pages 4 and 5 with them. Point out the main elements of the dictionary and discuss how to find information. Then read some of the "✐Dictionary Detective" activities and have students complete the challenge. For specific ideas on how to build phonics and language skills, read "Phonics Helps Build Reading Skills!" beginning on page 140. Also visit the web site noted below for wonderful activity sheets that you can download.

Internet Link to Language Development Activities

Please visit **www.ballard-tighe.com/picturedictionary.htm** for links to activities you can use with the *IDEA Picture Dictionary*. You will find fun activities that build vocabulary and phonics skills for elementary students as well as older students learning to read English.

▶ *Activities are provided at two levels so you can choose the ones appropriate for your students.*

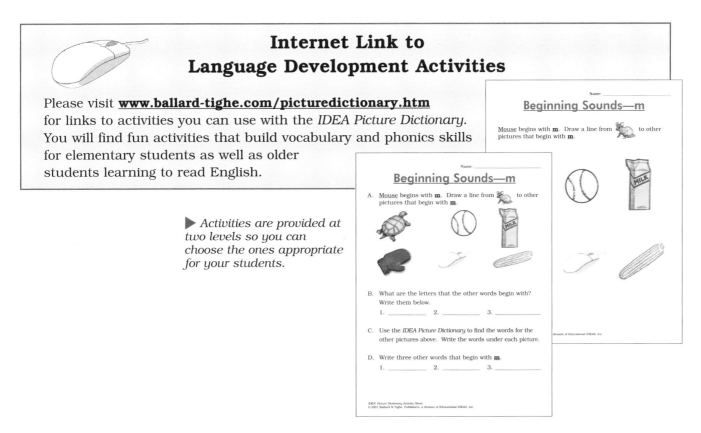

---

*Pronunciations are derived from the following three sources: *American Heritage College Dictionary, Third Edition*, 1997; *Oxford American Dictionary: Heald Colleges Edition*, 1986; and *Webster's New World College Dictionary, Fourth Edition*, 1999.

Phonics Helps Build Reading Skills!

Phonics is the process of attaching sounds (known as phonemes) to the letter or letters (graphemes) that represent those sounds. For example, if we know how to attach the /c/ /a/ /t/ sounds to the corresponding letters, we will be able to pronounce the printed word *cat*. By learning sound/symbol correspondences, students can pronounce words that may be unfamiliar to them. However, before students can make this connection between sounds and symbols, they must develop an understanding that language is made up of sounds that can be manipulated. This is called "phonemic awareness." Phonemic awareness is fundamental to reading. Read below how to help students build phonemic awareness and phonics skills. The ✎ icon indicates suggested activities to build each skill.

THE FIRST BUILDING BLOCKS—SOUNDS

The following activities will help students develop an understanding of sounds in language (i.e., phonemic awareness):

1. **What sounds do you hear in *cat*?** It is important for students to identify the sounds in spoken words (e.g., cat = /c/ /a/ /t/).

   ✎ Say words very slowly and ask students to listen for each sound. Emphasize a specific sound that you want students to focus on, such as /t/ in *bat*. Point out words familiar to students that have the same phonic element, such as *hat* and *cat*. As students begin to master this skill, you can extend the activity by giving students *IDEA Picture* cards of words such as *hat*, *cat*, *flag*, and *desk* and asking them to find all the words that end with the same sound.

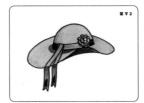   

▲ *Have students find the words that end with the same sound.*

2. **How many sounds do you hear?** Words contain different sounds. Some words have the same number of letters and sounds (e.g., *cat* has three letters and three sounds). Others, such as *dog* and *knob* have the same number of sounds, but a different number of letters.

   ✎ Give students practice "hearing" the sounds of words by having them clap as they hear the sounds in words. Then have students create personal dictionaries of words that contain one, two, or three (or more) sounds.

3. **What difference does a sound make?** One sound can mean the difference between *hit* and *it*! It is important for students to know that a sound or several sounds in a word can be deleted to create new words.

   ✎ Play "Do As I Say" with sounds. Give prompts such as "Do as I say; take the /b/ away from *bat*. Do as I say; take the /h/ away from *hand*."

▲ *Have students create personal dictionaries, such as the one above made with a pattern from Carousel of IDEAS.*

4. **Can you make a new word by changing sounds?** We can make entirely new words by deleting sounds, as previously noted, as well as by substituting sounds. For example, *rag* becomes *tag* when we substitute /t/ for /r/.

 Assign each student a sound, then pick a word such as *cake*. Point out the picture of cake in the *IDEA Picture Dictionary*. Ask each student in turn to replace the first sound in the word with his or her assigned sound to see if it makes a real word. You also can emphasize how sounds can be manipulated by identifying objects through rhyming words. Show a word from the *IDEA Picture Dictionary* or one of the *IDEA Picture* cards (e.g., pencil). Then say, "This is a tencil, fencil, pencil." Ask students to choose the word from the series that is the name of the picture.

5. **What makes these words similar?** Students must be able to identify the similarities in words. For example, what do /pen/, /pat/, and /pig/ have in common? [They all start with the /p/ sound!]

 Integrate alliteration into everyday tasks. For example, when doing oral work with students, ask someone to bring you "the **b**ig, **b**lue **b**owl." Or, before lining up for lunch, ask students to find objects in the room that begin with a certain sound; as each student responds, he or she moves to the line. You can use the *IDEA Picture Dictionary* to teach students how to incorporate alliteration in their own sentences. Ask them to go to a section in the dictionary, e.g., the "Ll" section, and create phrases and sentences that integrate alliteration. For example, "Lola loves lemon lollipops." Have a contest to see which student can use the most words in an alliterative way.

▲ "Bring me the **b**ig, **b**lue **b**owl."

6. **Can you hear this sound?** Isolating sounds enables students to identify specific elements such as the initial sounds of words.

 Show students a word such as *cow* in the *IDEA Picture Dictionary* or show an *IDEA Picture* card of the word. Ask students to say the first sound (/c/) and then pause before they say the rest of the word. When students master this, ask them to follow the same procedure for the final sound and then the medial sound.

7. **Does the cat wear a hat?** Rhyming demonstrates students' ability to hear relationships among words of similar sounds.

 Make poetry a part of every day. Read poems, create rhymes about everyday activities (e.g., Let's have a **look** at this pretty **book**.), or play a game of "I am thinking of a word that rhymes with ____" to emphasize the sameness of words. Show a picture(s) from the *IDEA Picture Dictionary* or an *IDEA Picture* card and ask students to create a rhyming sentence. Encourage students to create their own poetry, using the pronunciations in the *IDEA Picture Dictionary* to help them with sounds and the words to help them with correct spelling.

▲ *Rhyming activities are available at* <u>www.ballard-tighe.com/ picturedictionary.htm</u>.

8. **Do you want to play a /spl/endid game?** Phonemic blending allows students to put sounds together into a smoothly formed oral word.

 Begin with small blending units, even with multisyllabic words. Show pictures of words such as *president, brown, dress,* and *sheep* in the *IDEA Picture Dictionary*. Ask students to sound out each word. Then ask them to attack more challenging words, e.g., *splendid.* Begin with /sp/, /spl/, /splen/, and continue until they have sounded out the entire word *splendid*. Students can create personal picture dictionaries or posters showing the splendid words they can pronounce.

ANOTHER BUILDING BLOCK—CONNECTING SOUNDS AND SYMBOLS

As soon as students understand that language is made up of sounds they can manipulate, they are ready to connect the sounds to symbols—and to read! Phonics skills help students attack unfamiliar written words. Students must master the four major phonics skills listed below.

1. **Recognize which letters or letter combinations represent sounds.** Students need to know which letters or combinations of letters represent particular sounds. For example, they must recognize that /t/ is the same sound at the beginning of the words *tap* and *tame* and that *ough* represents different sounds in *though* and *tough*. Since phonics adds the visual dimension to the sounds developed in phonemic awareness, it is time to emphasize the word in written form.

   ✏ 1) Have students look at words in the *IDEA Picture Dictionary* that begin with the same letter. As they are looking at the written words, pronounce those words. This will emphasize the sound and the symbol that represents it. 2) Use word walls of words that have similar written elements but different pronunciations. Use these words in conversation and writing to solidify similarities and differences. 3) Create opportunities that give students continued exposure to words that have been presented orally. For example, give students various *IDEA Picture & Word* cards and ask them to put them into categories (e.g., according to beginning sounds or ending sounds). Students should be asked to use the words orally and in writing.

2. **Blending the individual sounds of a word together to form a true word.** Students must understand how to blend individual sounds to create words. For example, a student must be able to pronounce the individual sounds /f/ /i/ /sh/ and then to put those sounds together to make the word *fish*. For some learners, blending sounds is very difficult.

   ✏ 1) Break words into smaller units or emphasize onset (initial letter or letters) and rhyme (remaining portion of the word). For example, ask students to say the beginning sound in the word *fish* (/f/). Then ask them what letter goes with the /f/ sound (f). Ask them to look up the word *fish* in the "Ff" section of the *IDEA Picture Dictionary*. Ask them to look at the word and pronounce the /f/ and then the /ish/ to produce *fish*. 2) Point out similar familiar words to build blending skills. For example, students who know the word *dish* will be better able to blend f-i-s-h.

   ▲ *Students must put the sounds /f/ /i/ /sh/ together to make the word* fish.

3. **Storing phonemes in their correct sequence.** Students must be able to produce sounds in the order in which the letters appear. Frequently students can attach sounds to individual letters one at a time, but are unable to then reproduce those sounds in the correct order. For example, a student may pronounce /r/ /i/ /p/ as individual sounds and then say the word as *pit* or *pear*.

   ✏ 1) Have students use letter tiles to place the letters in sequence as they pronounce the sounds of a word. 2) Give students an *IDEA Word* card and allow them to move their fingers under the word so they point to each letter or letter combination. 3) Sometimes with emergent readers or those who have perceptual difficulties, it may be necessary to mark the first letter with a dot or color code it to stress its placement in the word. Remember that after students have sounded out the unfamiliar word, they need to say the word smoothly as a whole unit for it to become part of their vocabulary.

4. **Completing a memory search that matches phoneme combinations with real words that are part of their conceptual (meaning) vocabulary.** While phonics is often critical to word attack, comprehension is the ultimate objective of reading. Students may attach the correct sounds to the letters in a word such as *cove* but if they have no understanding of what a cove is, the reading act is not complete.

   ✏ 1) Use the *IDEA Picture Dictionary* to point out the pictures of words. Seeing the word and picture emphasizes the connection between objects and printed words. 2) Use multisensory stimuli to be sure that words on the page are

Label the farm animals.
Use the words below.

chicken	cow	goat
rooster	goose	bee
ant	sheep	turkey
chick	colt	pig
calf	horse	duck
	lamb	butterfly

Bonus Question: Name all the animals above that lay eggs.

▲ *Activities like this help students put new words in context. Download this activity sheet at* www.ballard-tighe.com/ picturedictionary.htm.

connected to ideas. Give students a chance to hear and see the word, trace it, write it in their notebook, and so forth. 3). Refer to the *IDEA Picture Dictionary* often to underscore its use as a reference tool and as a natural part of the students' learning strategy.

TIPS TO MAKE LANGUAGE DEVELOPMENT MORE EFFECTIVE AND FUN!

Dictionaries are excellent tools to reinforce the meaning of words. They are critical tools for students, especially those learning a new language. Here are severals tips to make language development—oral language as well as reading and writing—more effective and fun!

* Provide as much oral language as possible. Phonics is a sound-based system that needs oral reinforcement to be effective. In the classroom, students must have opportunities to hear and see the language in order to become proficient readers. Read stories, tell jokes, use audiotapes, have conversations, and ask open-ended questions. Encourage students to interview neighbors or classroom visitors, tell stories on the way to lunch, or point out objects while you describe them. Many, varied experiences with oral language are critical to reading success.

* Encourage students to experiment with language. Students who are just beginning the reading process and those who are having reading difficulties tend to apply the same sound whenever they see a letter. Encourage students to try various sounds and sound combinations until the word "sounds" like a real word to them. If they have difficulty using this "trial and error" approach, you may need to give them a "plan of attack" such as first use the short vowel sound, then try the long vowel, now try vowel combinations, and so forth. Emphasize that they have many strategies and tools to aid in their reading and writing, including this dictionary.

* Use manipulatives. The *IDEA Picture Dictionary*, *IDEA Picture & Word* cards, letter tiles, blocks, moveable letters, marking boards, erasers, and other manipulatives help students to develop phonics skills. Since the brain stores information in multiple places, it is critical to provide students with as much varied sensory input as possible to tap all areas of the brain. Encouraging students to see, hear, feel, and touch letters will enable them to tap various storage areas of the brain. A phonics skill such as exchanging one sound for another is a sophisticated activity. However, the task is much "simpler" when a letter is physically removed and another letter is put in its place using letter cards or other manipulatives.

* Link to prior learning. Students must attach new learning to prior knowledge. For example, if students already know how to read the word *cute,* they can relate that knowledge to attack an unfamiliar word such as *chute.* Remind students of the relationships between words they already know to ones that are unfamiliar to them. Making word walls or dictionaries of words that rhyme (e.g., cute, chute, brute) or contain similar phonic elements (e.g., lamb, comb, crumb) will encourage students to relate familiar words with new ones.

* Apply phonics learning frequently in authentic settings. Often, students can attack words in isolation (e.g., *cloak*), but have difficulty reading the word correctly in a sentence (e.g., The princess put her cloak around her shoulders.). Students must see the application of phonics in many settings (e.g., on word cards, on practice pages, in their readers) and practice them often in order for the sound/symbol relationships to become familiar. If students encounter the /ai/ combination often enough, they will recognize that combination when it appears in more complex words such as *remain.* Just because students have mastered the sound in the short term does not mean that the sound is permanently a part of their word attack repertoire. Students should see the new words in print (e.g., on word cards, on the board, in a sentence), hear the new words, and write the new words.

(continued)

* Introduce sounds in context. Introduce the sounds of the English language in context and provide examples of words that have those sounds. For example, /t/ is what we hear at the beginning of *toe*, *trumpet*, and *tiger*. Encourage students to make dictionaries, create word walls, use egg cartons to house pictures and/or words with similar elements, or make scrapbooks of pictures and words. This will help students understand how to apply the sounds. These activities also reinforce the connection between sounds and the letters that represent them.

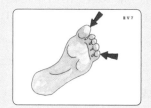

▲ *Readers need exposure to words in many settings such as word cards, practice pages, and readers.*

* Encourage students to write. Reading and writing are different sides of the same literacy coin. Students who write as they learn phonics tend to read faster and better than those who do not. This is especially true when students are encouraged to utilize personalized spelling for words that may not be part of their writing vocabulary. For example, writers who are willing to attempt to spell *tight* by producing *tite* or *tiet* are more likely to succeed in phonics than those who are reluctant to take such risks. Practice in producing the written form of words is an excellent way to both apply multisensory practice and demonstrate the relationship between sounds and the letters that represent them.

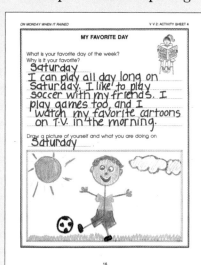

▲ *Give students many opportunities to write. The student work above comes from an IDEAS for Literature student journal.*

* Consider the students' native language. Students who are not native English speakers may encounter great difficulties with English. This is particularly true for students whose native language is not alphabetic (e.g., Chinese) or whose language is very phonetic (e.g., Spanish). Teachers need to focus on key phonics components and provide opportunities for English learners to practice seeing and hearing the sounds and letters. Moving too quickly from one new sound to another will confuse students and interfere with the mastery necessary to learn the elements. Provide visuals, such as *IDEA Picture & Word* cards, as well as actions to solidify a concept or word meaning and to make sure students hear and see the target words. You can help learners make the connections between ideas and words. Begin with pictures of simple, concrete words (e.g., *cat*, *house*, *tree*) and then move to more abstract ones (e.g., *government*, *helpers*, *structure*).